Parenting

RABBI RAMI
GUIDE TO

Parenting

WITH **AGAPI THEODOROU**

--- Roadside Assistance for the Spiritual Traveler ---

Spirituality
&**Health**
BOOKS

Rabbi Rami Guide to Parenting:
Roadside Assistance for the Spiritual Traveler
By Rami Shapiro

© 2011 Rami Shapiro

Spirituality
& **Health**
BOOKS

425 Boardman Street, Suite C
Traverse City, MI 49684
www.spiritualityhealth.com

Printed in Canada.

Cover and interior design by Sandra Salamony

Cataloging-in-Publication data for this book is available
upon request.

978-0-9837270-1-9
10 9 8 7 6 5 4 3 2 1

CONTENTS

Who Am I and
Where Did I Come From?

Where Am I Going?

What Am I Here To Do?

Why?

Summary

INTRODUCTION

I'M NOT DR. SPOCK, Dr. Oz, or Dr. Phil. I don't know anything special about potty training, early-childhood development, or family dynamics. While it's true I no longer crap in my pants, this may change as I get older. And as far as nutrition and all other relevant parenting subjects go, my being overweight and as crazy as the next fellow certainly doesn't attest to my expertise. The only credibility I have regarding parenting is that I am a parent, and any guy with a functioning penis of a certain age and level of virility can do that.

I am a Ph.D. as well as a rabbi, however, so you can add Dr. Rami to the Spock, Oz, and Phil list, but I teach Bible rather than human development, and, in case you haven't noticed, the Bible's tips on parenting are less than stellar:

Adam and Eve's firstborn, Cain, kills his younger brother in a fit of jealous rage (Genesis 4:8), and while we can't always blame parents for the murderous behavior of their children, one can't help wondering.

Abraham sends his first son, Ishmael, off to die with his mother in the desert (Genesis 21:14), and years later sets out to murder his second son, Isaac, in an act of child sacrifice to God (Genesis 22:1–14).

Lot, Abe's nephew, is raped by his two daughters who are too lazy to walk over to the next town to meet guys and make babies (Genesis 19:30–36), and Tamar, the widowed wife of Judah's son Er, dresses up as a prostitute and seduces her recently widowed father-in-law and has twins by him (Genesis 38:1–30).

God tells moms and dads that they can stone to death a rebellious son (Deuteronomy 21:18–21), and Jephtah, one of the Judges of Israel, kills his daughter to fulfill a vow he made to God.

And that's just the Hebrew Bible. Turn to the Gospels and we discover that Jesus never talks to his human dad; his mother thinks he's insane (Mark 3:21); he seems to tell us to hate our moms and dads (Luke 14:26); he rejects his own mother (Mark 3:31–35); Jesus' heavenly Dad is intent on killing him (Luke 22:42), and abandons him as he dies (Matthew 27:46). All in all, if I'm looking for a book on parenting, the Good Book isn't all that good at it.

So this is definitely not a book about Bible family

values. So what, if anything, does a rabbi, even one with a Ph.D., know that is applicable to parenting? I would say two things: asking questions and telling stories.

Judaism is all about asking questions and telling stories. In fact, we often ask questions just so we can tell stories. Why, for example, after Abraham sacrifices a ram to God rather than his son Isaac, does Abraham return to his waiting servants without Isaac? He tells them before leaving for the sacrifice that he and Isaac will return to them after the sacrifice (Genesis 22:5), and yet only Abraham returns (Genesis 22:19). Where's Isaac? The Bible doesn't say, so we Jews fill in the blank by telling stories. In Hebrew, we call these stories *midrash* (to seek out, investigate). Stories help us investigate and seek out meaning in the blank spaces of our lives.

For example, perhaps Isaac, who according to Jewish tradition is thirty-three years old when this event happens, decides that he is safer not traveling with dad for a while. Or perhaps, he suddenly remembers what Abe did to Ishmael, Isaac's half-brother, and sets off to find Ishmael and reconcile with him. This makes sense, since we see Isaac and Ishmael together at their father's funeral (Genesis 25:11).

The point is, we don't know. And when we don't know, we tell stories.

What does storytelling have to do with parenting? Everything. The biggest unknown in a parent's life is her child. These beings come into the world without papers. We have no idea who they are, where they came from, what they are supposed to do, where they are going, or why they exist at all. So we make up stories: stories about them and stories about ourselves; stories about nature, about life, death, and afterlife; stories about fate, karma, destiny, heavens and hells, and rewards and punishments. And we tell these stories to our kids. Except we don't tell them they are stories. We offer them with the same matter-of-factness that we use when we tell them that breakfast is the most important meal of the day, and not to take candy from strangers. The stories we tell our kids shape them far more profoundly than the rules we set for them. Here is a true story about rules:

Many years ago my congregation held a party on Miami Beach. My then five-year-old son ran around the beach with his friends building and smashing sand castles. He wore a regular bathing suit, a T-shirt, and a six-shooter. My son always packed heat. It wasn't a real gun, of course, and he wasn't allowed to point it at anyone, but he wore it and shot imaginary bad guys when the mood took him or the need arose.

I was raised the same way. Every year on the first night of Hanukkah, my parents presented me with a new gun and holster set. We weren't an especially violent family, and my plastic gun fetish didn't turn me into a right-wing militia member planning to "take back America." As I grew older the guns stopped coming, and they, along with my Fess Parker coonskin cap, eventually went to the Goodwill. So I didn't worry about my son's love of toy guns.

The same cannot be said for one of my congregants. A woman somewhat older than myself came storming over to me incensed over my gun-toting kid. She was appalled that a rabbi would allow his son to carry weapons. I made the mistake of defending myself.

I suggested that if Jews had been trained to carry guns in their *tallis* bags along with their prayer shawls (*tallis*), we might have thwarted the Nazis the way we did the Persians in the story of Esther. She had no idea what the story of Esther was—my bad—and was not convinced. I then suggested the guns were training for my son's eventual move to Israel where he would join the IDF, the Israeli Defense Force, but this, too, had little effect. I finally resorted to paraphrasing the NRA: Guns don't kill, obnoxious Jewish mothers do. That unfortunately only escalated matters.

By this time other members of my congregation had assembled to watch what could only end badly. Lucky for me the woman's two sons, then in high school, were among the gathering throng. As their mother lectured me on how she never allowed her boys to have toy guns, the boys interrupted her: "You may not have allowed us to have toy guns, but we made them all the time. We had stick guns, straw guns, finger guns. We shot everyone and everything. We loved guns!"

A hush fell over the crowd. The woman herself was stunned. I imagined that she wished she had a gun at that very moment. Her mouth opened and closed several times. She clearly wanted to speak, but could not. She turned a deep and angry purple and stormed off. In my mind I shot here with a finger gun.

The crowd dispersed—"Move along, people. There's nothing more to see here"—and the moment passed. The woman quit the congregation, and I never heard from her again.

The moral of this story: your kids are going to do what your kids are going to do, and you don't have all that much control over them. Sure, when they are little, you can bully them; after all, you are bigger than they are. But don't imagine this will stick. Eventually they will either simply ignore you or find a therapist who will help them get over you.

I'm not saying you shouldn't set rules for your children. I'm only saying that you should also expect them to break those rules. But I could be wrong about all of this. Like I said, I'm a storyteller, not a parenting expert, but the Bible backs me up.

The first Dad was God. Adam and Eve were His kids. And He had only one rule in His household: "Don't eat from the Tree of Knowledge of Good and Evil. Other than that, kids, have a good time." So what did they do? Of course they ate from the Tree of Knowledge of Good and Evil.

What else would they do? What else would you do?

My mom used to play mah jong every Wednesday night when I was young. She and "the girls" would rotate hosting the game, and one Wednesday evening a month for fifteen years I would fall asleep with the sound of clacking tiles and Mom and her friends calling out, "One Bam, two Crack" or something like that.

During the afternoon on those Wednesdays the game was to come to our house, my mom would bake a cake and chocolate chip cookies for her friends to eat while they played. When my sister and I came home from school, she would always remind us, "You may freely eat of every tree of the garden; but of the tree of the knowledge of good and evil you shall not eat, for in the day that you eat of it you shall die" (Genesis 2:16–17). Well, that is what God said to Adam; my mom said something more akin to, "These cookies are for the girls. If you take one I will kill you."

Like Pavlov's dog, I was raised to respond to certain stimuli. In this case, the forbidden cookie. There was plenty of food to eat in our house, and much of it was just as empty of nutritional value as those cookies, but it was the forbidden chip that I craved above all else.

When my mother was distracted I would study the layout of the cookies on the plate, seeking to discern which ones could be eaten and which others could be repositioned to mask the fact that some had been eaten. Satisfied that I knew which to eat and which to shift, I waited for just the right moment to steal the cookies. I usually stole one for myself and another for my sister. It wasn't that I loved my sister so much, but that I, like Adam, hoped to share the blame if caught.

More often than not we got away with the theft, and when we were caught, Mom, like Adam and Eve's Dad, didn't kill us but banished us from the kitchen to our rooms. We went with a smile on our faces and our tongues searching for cookie crumbs in the corners of our mouths.

You might take the story of Adam and Eve eating from the Tree of Knowledge of Good and Evil more seriously than I do. I have some friends who believe that because of the sin of the first people, all subsequent people are doomed to eternal torment in hell, and that God had to send His Son, Jesus, to die on the cross so that those of us who accept Him as God can escape the punishment God will otherwise mete out on those who do not.

I marvel at the seriousness with which they take these Jewish stories. My mom didn't have another son to sacrifice to save my sister and me from her wrath, though I have met parents who do triangulate among their children, punishing one for the sins of the others. But my point isn't what parents do with the stories they tell, but that all parents tell stories as a way of shaping the lives of their children.

The reason I'm writing this brief *Guide to Parenting* is because I think storytelling rather than rule making is the key to good parenting. It is the stories we tell our kids, not the rules, that will stay with them—for good or for ill—for the rest of their lives.

The stories I'm talking about aren't just "once upon a time" stories, the stories you read to your children at bedtime. The stories I'm talking about include the more subtle stories, the stories we pretend aren't stories at all, but facts, truths, and inescapable realities. The *Rabbi Rami Guide to Parenting* will address both kinds of stories: the ones we tell and the ones we read, but it is the former that will occupy us the most.

Here are just a few such stories I have heard in the past week:

> "I am a Jew, a member of God's Chosen
> People, and because we are chosen, other
> people, people not chosen by God, hate us,
> hate me. Even when they appear nice, Gentiles
> hate Jews. I never trust them. And if any of my

kids married one, I'd sit *shiva* for them. They
would be dead to me."

Shiva is the seven-day Jewish mourning period.
Most Jews mourn when a person actually dies, but
some, like the mother who said this to me, will consider their children dead if they disobey them and
marry someone not of the Jewish faith.

> "Most people are going to hell. They may
> be nice people and all, they may even think
> they are Christians and are going to Heaven
> because they are Christians, but most people—
> billions really—are going to burn in hell for all
> eternity. That's God's plan, and He determined
> who is going to burn even before they were
> born. There's nothing you can do about it. The
> only way you know you are one of the few
> bound for heaven is that you know that most
> are bound for hell. It is a feeling deep inside. I
> have it, thank God."

This is a story told by many of my students at
Middle Tennessee State, a bastion of Calvinist thinking in the buckle of the Bible Belt. Calvinists believe

in determinism: God has decided whether or not you will be saved before you are ever born. It isn't a choice, but a surrender to your fate, or what they call the "irresistible grace" of God. Even if you want to believe in Jesus as Christ, even if you attest to this belief, if you are not predestined for heaven by God, you are going to hell.

> "We are born to be healthy, wealthy, and happy. What keeps us from these things is our habit of thinking negatively. People get sick because they think sick thoughts. Breast cancer comes from being angry. Throat cancer comes because you don't speak your truth. Poor people think poverty and stay poor. People who get robbed or raped or even murdered all attracted these things into their lives by their thoughts. Everyone gets what he or she thinks about. Think rich, get rich. That's my motto."

I often teach at so-called New Age centers, and this is the kind of story I hear there. Everything depends on the quality of our thoughts, and we can read the quality of our thoughts by reading the kinds of emotions we are having. If we feel good, we are thinking good; if we feel bad, we are thinking bad.

These are the kinds of stories I am concerned with in this book; the stories that shape our lives and determine the kinds of people we will be. We don't invent these stories by ourselves; we learn them from others. Whether you work at it or not, chances are your child will outgrow diapers and learn to use the toilet. But if you don't work at it, chances are your child will pick up stories that may make her life needlessly miserable.

You may agree or disagree with the three stories just mentioned. They are just three that stuck out in my mind when I thought back over the conversations I have had in the past seven days with people in various settings. They aren't meant to be definitive; they're simply examples of the kinds of stories we will be talking about—the kind that define lives.

Like midrash, stories, especially the life-defining kinds of stories, are told to fill in the unknown in our lives. The unknown is often hinted at in the questions these stories come to answer. There are five of these existential questions and, hence, five kinds of stories that we will deal with in this book. Here are the five questions:

> *Who am I?*
> *Where did I come from?*
> *Where am I going?*
> *What am I here to do?*
> *Why?*

Most of the *Rabbi Rami Guide to Parenting* is devoted to these five questions, and examples of stories that I believe answer them in ways that produce spiritually healthy girls and boys. I won't be telling the stories that lead to spiritually unhealthy children, though I may reference one or two. The reason for this is simple: the negative stories are all too prevalent, and trying to root them out is far too difficult. Rather than eradicate the negative stories, I hope to guide you to tell the positive stories, and in this way minimize the effects of the negative stories that your children will inevitably hear.

Of course the stories I will tell to answer the questions just asked may or may not suit you. If you do like my stories, use them and add to them with supportive stories from your family and your faith. If you don't like them, use this guide as a template: identify the stories you feel matter, articulate and share those stories with your child, and work to live those stories with your child through whatever spiritual practices or religious rituals you see fit. I am less concerned with you telling my stories than I am with you recognizing the power of story and telling your own. Think of this book as a model to be adapted rather than a cookbook to be followed.

And yet there is one caveat: do your best to not tell unhealthy stories. An unhealthy story is a story that leaves your children feeling superior to others, or frightened of others who are different from themselves. An unhealthy story is one that excuses violence, exploitation, the dehumanization of people, or inhumane treatment of animals. An unhealthy story is one that places your children in a world of perpetual conflict where friendship is rare if not impossible, where love is limited, where race, religion, creed, and ethnicity determine the value of a person rather than what she does, where collaboration is dismissed as starry-eyed idealism, and competition and hoarding are praised over cooperation and sharing. In short, spiritually healthy stories are those that teach your

23

children to "do justly, love mercy, and walk humbly" (Micah 6:8), and "love your neighbor as yourself" (Leviticus 19:18).

Sometimes it is hard to tell if a story is healthy or not. Take, for example, *The Giving Tree* by Shel Silverstein. People seem to love this story. I generally like Shel Silverstein stories, especially *The Missing Piece*, but I hate *The Giving Tree*. Here's why:

The Giving Tree is about a lady tree and her relationship with a boy whose narcissism is surpassed only by his capacity to exploit the tree. The tree gives of herself until she is nothing more than a stump. The boy just takes and takes, and while he does grow old, he never grows up. The message of this story: your life has value only to the extent you are willing to sacrifice it for others, even the most selfish.

There are moments when self-sacrifice, even the extreme self-sacrifice of dying to save another, is warranted. But sacrificing yourself for people like the boy in this book makes the tree into a stump and you into a chump.

Shel's *The Missing Piece* is something else entirely. In this story a Pac-Man-shaped character is looking for the missing pie slice that will make him whole.

Given his missing piece, he sort of hobbles around slowly, having plenty of time to befriend the world he encounters. He tries many different pieces but none fits. Then one day he happens on just the right-sized piece and he is made perfectly round. Now he rolls faster and faster and cannot appreciate anything in the rush of gathering speed. Luckily he hits something, and his missing piece is knocked out and lost. Far wiser, he then continues his search for the missing piece, with a wink—knowing that, rather than preventing him from living, it is his lack that allows him to live.

This is a healthy story. It tells us that we all have a sense of lack, a wound, a missing something that we imagine would make us so happy if we could but find it. Our search for what is missing takes us into the world, and because we are wounded we can befriend the world, for everything is wounded. It is only when we are perfect that things go awry. The message is this: true wholeness includes absence; true completeness includes brokenness. If you want to live well in the world, if you want to enjoy life and befriend the living, don't seek to escape your brokenness, but use it to slow down and embrace others.

• • •

The first half of the *Rabbi Rami Guide to Parenting* focuses on the Five Questions and the five kinds of stories you might tell regarding them. Along with my generic stories and exercises, I will mention children's books that I believe support those stories, which I urge you to read to your children.

The second half of this *Guide* will take up each of these stories, along with some others, offering you a short synopsis highlighting the moral of the story, and a brief rationale as to why you might want to read this story to your child.

While I had a hand in choosing the stories, I turned for advice and the actual writing of this section to Agapi Theodorou, a Ph.D. candidate in children's literature at Middle Tennessee State University. Our list of stories is not definitive; we offer it only to help you get started. There are lots of wonderful children's books out there. Find those that speak to your values and share them with your children. But more importantly, pay attention to the other stories you tell your children: the stories that don't come in books, but through your own life and behavior. Take care that

these stories point your child toward a healthy understanding of life and a welcoming attitude toward all
who live it.

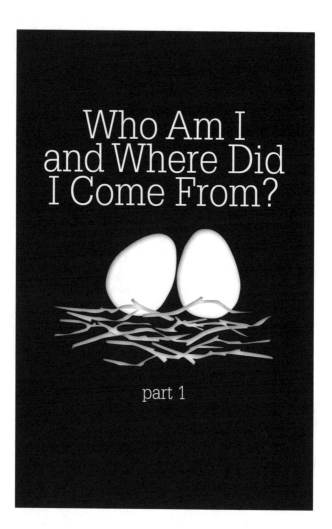

Who Am I and Where Did I Come From?

part 1

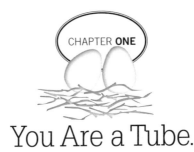

CHAPTER ONE

You Are a Tube.

THE FIRST TWO of the five existential questions we shall ask and answer in this *Guide* are so closely related that it is best to link them and answer them together.

Let's start with a concrete answer about what you are: you are a body. And what is this body? It is basically a tube, not so different from that of a worm. Food goes in at one end, waste comes out at the other, and in between all kinds of cool things happen.

The body is so complex that even the doctors on *House* usually need the entire time allotted to them between commercials to figure out what is wrong with their patient. And even when they do, the patient sometimes dies anyway. While it may be gratifying to the doctors to know why a person dies, chances are the person doing the dying is more concerned with the dying part.

Anyway, that is about all I know regarding the

body: it's a tube that does cool things and then dies, often in horrible ways. The amount of time allotted for doing cool things is sometimes quite short and sometimes quite long. If we take care of this tube—eat right and exercise, that kind of thing—we might extend the time the body has to do cool things, but I've known too many people—people who ate well and exercised regularly who still died young—to believe that we have that much control over the fate of this tube.

Still, I would recommend eating well and exercising daily, if only to optimize the cool things your body does as long as it does them. So feed your kids well and help them develop an active lifestyle.

To help with the first, I suggest you read *Food Rules: An Eater's Manual* by Michael Pollan. Among Michael's rules are these that I find very helpful:

> **RULE #11:** Avoid foods you see advertised on television.

> **RULE #19:** If it comes from a plant, eat it; if it is made in a plant, don't.

> **RULE #36:** Don't eat breakfast cereals that change the color of the milk.

When it comes to exercise, I cannot say enough about team sports. Most of it bad. Not that there is anything wrong with team sports—there isn't—it's just that my dad obsessed over my being a team player, and I'm not.

I'm a loner. I like being alone. I like reading alone, eating alone, walking alone. And when I spend time with people it is either because I choose to or I am paid to do so. Which still involves choice. Anyway, I mention this only to say that you should allow your kid to be who she is rather than who my dad wanted her to be.

Most kids want to please their parents; at least when they're young. It was easy to please my mom: just the fact I was breathing made her happy. My dad was a bit more demanding. He played first base in the army during World War II. When he wasn't firing artillery shells at Nazis, he was catching baseballs; and while he did everything he could to see that I didn't have to deal with Nazis, he was dead set on my learning how to catch a baseball. Not a bad goal if your tube has a capacity for catching baseballs, but a long horror if it doesn't.

I was drafted into Little League and played for the

Grays. Left field, as I recall. Most of the time nothing happened in left field, and that was fine with me. What I hated was batting. My bat always seemed too thin, and it rarely connected with a pitched ball. I needed a thick bat like the one Bam-Bam carried in *The Flintstones*, but that was against the rules.

The one time I hit a pitch and ran to first base, I tripped and fell flat on my face midway between home plate and first base. Lucky for me the kid who picked up my ground ball as it scooted past the shortstop threw it to first for the out rather than to home to stop the winning run from scoring. Given the esoteric mysteries of baseball, I actually won the game for my team, but I was still humiliated. My dad was a good sport about it though and raced out from the stands to see if I was hurt.

In high school I was expected to earn my school letter (an "L" for Longmeadow) through sports. I could have earned it by being features editor on the school newspaper, a job I held for two years, but that didn't count. So I went out for varsity baseball. I was picked to be the towel boy.

I also tried out for basketball. I was made the announcer.

I made it on to the wrestling team, but being that close to sweating male bodies was too much for me, and I quit.

I once unofficially broke the school record for discus, but when it came to doing it again officially, I got dizzy and dropped it just inches from my feet.

So, while I did earn my "L" for laundering the sweat-soaked towels of the baseball players, I have no real love of team sports. This doesn't mean you shouldn't encourage your kids to play sports, only that if they really hate it, don't wait until they develop a psychosomatic illness to get out of playing before you stop pestering them. I no longer have that illness, though I still get panic attacks upon seeing a large pile of sweat-soaked towels.

In addition to any team sports you might sign your kid up for, I would suggest you get them into things like walking, hiking, yoga, tai–chi, and Pilates as well. What I like about these sports is that they are life-long endeavors. You can play football for only so long before your tube just gives out. In my case "so long" was the first week of my freshman year of college.

Still trying to impress my dad, I had signed up to take football for my physical education credit. First day, first game, first play of the game, the other team kicked off and the ball came straight toward me. I made the mistake of catching it and carrying it toward their goal posts. By the time the refs got the other team off of me, my leg was broken and I was out for the season. And this was flag football! I never went back.

On the other hand, you see a lot of healthy middle-aged people walking in Centrum® Silver commercials, and tai-chi seems very good for old Chinese people, and yoga guru B.K.S. Iyengar is still stretching at ninety-four or so, so I suggest you introduce your kids to these exercises early.

Of course these activities can be dangerous as well. I love to walk and once walked into a rattlesnake den in Austin, Texas. And on a hike in the redwoods in Northern California I bumped into a mountain lion; and a walk in a park in New Delhi brought me face to horns with a Brahma bull who was none too happy to see me. But I survived all three encounters and they make for good stories over dinner.

Exercise cannot guarantee you long life, of course, and not exercising doesn't guarantee a short one either. My mother-in-law lived well into her seventies as a lifelong chain smoker whose only sport was miniature golf. I tried that as well (miniature golf, not smoking), but the windmill defeated me every time.

So eat well and exercise regularly, not because it will keep you alive longer, but because for most of us it will make the life you have better for as long as you have it, which, even when it is long, isn't really all that long.

Think about that for a moment. Humans have been around for hundreds of thousands of years, but chances are you and your kids won't make it past 120. Given the grand scheme of things, your life is little more than a blip on the cosmic screen, and yet it is such a precious blip. That is the story you have to teach your children regarding the body—it is precious.

This is what I want children to know about their bodies: they are wondrous tubes capable of doing magnificent things if well maintained and treated with respect. Because this is the message I want them to learn, I do my best to avoid telling them stories that degrade their body or the bodies of others, and I do my best to find stories to tell them that honor the body and speak to how best to treat it.

35

As shocking as it is every time I encounter it, I know lots of people, some of whom are parents, who don't think the body is precious at all. In fact, some of them hate the body in general, and their bodies and their children's bodies in particular.

During a conversation on circumcision I once had with a married couple about to have their first child, a boy, the mom said, "I'm totally in favor of circumcision. In fact, if it were up to me I'd cut the whole thing off."

"Excuse me," I said, not sure I was following her thought.

"The penis. I'd cut the whole wicked little sucker off right from the start. I hate the damn thing. All women do."

Actually, all women don't, but this woman clearly did. I looked to her husband who was staring into the back of his hands strategically positioned to protect his penis if the need should arise. He looked ashamed, but I couldn't tell if he was ashamed of his wife or ashamed of his penis or the fact that he had one.

I suggested that this woman get therapy, and that her animosity toward the penis was perhaps—I'm not Dr. Phil—indicative of animosity toward men in general, and that since she was having a son, she might want to do what she could to minimize the damage her hatred might do to his psyche. She told me to do something with my penis that is anatomically impossible and left with her husband in tow. I never saw her or her family again.

I know lots of guys who are ashamed of their bodies, and I may be among them. I want to look like Arnold Schwarzenegger, and instead I look like Oliver Hardy. I know lots of women who are ashamed of their bodies as well. While I can avoid watching old Arnold movies, and I left California partly to avoid having my governor mock my flabbiness every time he held a press conference, I don't see how any but Amish women can avoid being assaulted day in and day out by bodies only a plastic surgeon could love.

So what is your body story? Do you see your body as a magnificent and precious tube or as something to be beaten into submission or pared down into some cookie-cutter ideal? What will you tell your kids about their bodies?

I hope you tell them how amazing the human body is. Sure it's cool that babies are totally taken with their feet and toes, but just wait until you can tell your little ones about opposable thumbs! I think if you tell them stories about the preciousness of their bodies they may be less inclined to abuse them. After all, who sprays graffiti on a Fabergé egg?

As you tell your children stories about the preciousness of their bodies, you will naturally be inclined to also tell them about the preciousness of other bodies: human and otherwise. There are lots of precious tubes in the universe, and they all deserve our respect and care.

But before kids can grasp that, they really have to understand that their tube is precious. One way to do this is to celebrate elimination. You know, peeing and pooping. *Everyone Poops* by Taro Gomi, is a great book for this, as is *The Gas We Pass* by Shinta Cho. I suggest you read these and similar books with your kids, but I want to offer something more long lasting, as well.

THE PRAYER OF THE GRATEFUL TUBE

Judaism has a custom of offering a prayer of thanksgiving every time we pee or poop. The prayer is called *Asher Yatzar* ("The One Who fashions humankind"). What follows is my translation of the Hebrew for adults; I'll leave it up to you to translate this for your kids.

Blessed are You, Source and Substance of all
creation, Who fashions me with wisdom. You
bless me with a body of wondrous balance and
complexity, a dynamic mix of openings and
closings, fills and hollows, that open and close
in tune with need and necessity. If openings
should close; or that which is closed open
improperly, I could not survive. Yet over these
I have no control. I owe my very being to their
proper functioning, and I am made humble
and grateful with this knowing. I honor Your
gift by honoring my body and respecting its
promise. Blessed are You, Healer of all flesh,
Who blesses me with this precious form.

What I do, and what I am encouraging you to do,
is make copies of this prayer, adapting the language as
you see fit, frame them, and place one in every bathroom in your home. (Traditionally Jews place them
outside the bathroom.) Then train yourself and your
children to recite it after peeing and pooping. I real-
ize this might sound strange at first, but I have found
reciting prayer to be among the most profound spiritual practices I do every day. Sometimes twice a day.
Hallelujah!

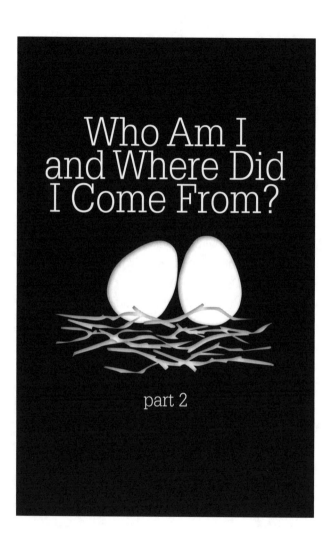

Who Am I and Where Did I Come From?

part 2

You Are the World and You Are from the World/Universe.

WHILE IT IS TRUE that we are tubes, it is also true that we are more than tubes.

Most of us were told the story that "I am my body." True enough. But what exactly is this body? Or better, where is it? Bodies are fascinating and kids love to look into the guts of our tubes.

When I was a kid I had Visible Man and Visible Woman toy models. These were large clear plastic figures that contained all the inner parts of our anatomy. You could remove the plastic shell and take out the parts to get a feel of how weird and wonderful the human tube is—although, based on these toys, I didn't know about penises and vaginas for years. (The same can be said of my friends who learned about human anatomy from Barbie and Ken dolls.)

I misremembered the name of these dolls as "Invisible" rather than "Visible," so when I tried to find these toys online, I failed: Invisible Man led me to novels by Ralph Ellison and H.G. Wells, and Invisible Woman turned out to be Sue Storm of the Fantastic Four. The Visible Man and Woman are indeed still available for about twenty dollars online. I also recommend getting a copy of *The Visual Dictionary of the Human Body*. This book is a wonderful celebration of the preciousness and awesomeness of our human tube.

As cool as the Visible Man and Woman are, they still have a problem (besides the fact that they lack genitalia): they tell an incomplete story—that we are what is inside our skins only. This is not true, and I suggest you tell a more complete story as answer to the question "Who am I?"

Take your lungs, for example, while they do exist inside your tube, and while they are absolutely essential to your survival, they rely on processes that have nothing to do with what goes on inside your body.

Lungs need oxygen, but they don't make oxygen.

While your body is good at making methane, and seems to get better at this with age, nothing in your body makes oxygen. Oxygen is made through the process of photosynthesis, a process that requires trees, plants, and sunlight. If your body needs lungs, and your lungs need oxygen, and oxygen needs trees and sunlight, then trees and sunlight are as essential to your body as your lungs. In fact, if you tell your kids the true story of their bodies, trees, plants, and sunlight are as much a part of their body as lungs.

Nor does the body end there. Trees need earth and water to survive, and sunlight needs the sun, so the planet earth and the sun are part of your body as well. For the earth and sun to be in just the right relationship for photosynthesis to happen and oxygen to be made, they need all the other planets and moons in our solar system to be just where they are so that gravity will hold the earth at just the right distance from the sun so that your tube doesn't freeze up or melt down. So the whole solar system is your body no less than your lungs. And the solar system needs the Milky Way Galaxy and the galaxy needs the universe so if the story of the body is well told, you discover that you are the universe. How's that for precious?

In addition to Visible Man, Visible Woman, and *The Visual Dictionary of the Human Body,* get a copy of *Planet Earth: As You've Never Seen It Before* by Alastair Fothergill, and *The Kids Book of the Night Sky* by Ann Love, Jane Drake, and Heather Collins, and help your children explore their larger body: the planet earth and solar system, as well.

Looking at pictures together and using these to tell the larger story of "you, the precious tube" is a wonderful thing to do with your children. But I would be remiss if I left off one more thing to do to tell this story—something I have done with hundreds of kids and parents all across the United States.

PLAY–DOH AND ARISTOTLE

Aristotle was born in Chalcidice in northern Greece in 384 BCE. Play-Doh was born in 1956. Aristotle's dad was a doctor, and I expect his parents wanted him to be one as well when he grew up. Play-Doh's parents were Noah and Joseph McVickers (yes, Play-Doh had two daddies) and they hoped their baby would be wallpaper cleaner. Ah, the disappointments of parenthood.

Aristotle grew up to be a philosopher, and Play-Doh

grew up to be a ubiquitous child's toy. While Judaism, Christianity, and Islam did their best to fit Aristotle into their respective theologies, his notion that the world was uncreated and eternal was always problematic. Don't let this bother you, however. Chances are your kid isn't going to ask about neo-Aristotelians such as Augustine, Maimonides, or al-Kindi any time soon. If you want to get your kids to fall asleep, you might try reading Aristotle's *Metaphysics* to them at night. It works well with adults, too.

Anyway, Aristotle taught that the world was eternal, and he couldn't accept the notion of creation *ex nihilo*, something from nothing. (Based on this, chances are he wouldn't have fallen for Bernie Madoff's pyramid scheme either.) Jewish, Christian, and Muslim religious teachers who came to believe in something from nothing had to either twist themselves or Aristotle into knots in order to agree, or simply agree to disagree and move on to other parts of Aristotle's philosophy with which they did agree.

I am talking about Aristotle for two reasons. First, I couldn't resist the pun in the subheading. Come on, Play-Doh and Aristotle—is that clever or what? It would make a great T-shirt—a can of Play-Doh next to a bust of Aristotle—and if you make one, please send me an extra-large. Or, if you don't get around to it for a few months, double X.

The second reason is a bit more serious: do we come from nothing or from something? Or, to put things more simply: are earthlings natural to earth or alien to her? If you are like me and like to know what the Bible has to say about things, you are in luck: the Bible says both things. You can't lose.

If you think humans are plopped onto humus from somewhere else, you'll love Genesis 1:26:

> Then God said, "Let us make humankind in
> our image, according to our likeness; and
> let them have dominion over the fish of the
> sea, and over the birds of the air, and over
> the cattle, and over all the wild animals of
> the earth, and over every creeping thing
> that creeps upon the earth." So God created
> humankind in his image, in the image of God
> he created them; male and female he created
> them. (Genesis 1:26–27, NRSV)

In this version of humanity's creation, we, like everything else in Chapter 1 of Genesis, are created *ex nihilo* (out of nothing): God decides and we reside. We are not indigenous to the planet earth, but are plopped onto it from outside of it in order to have dominion over it. God is, in a sense, the absentee landlord of the planet earth, and we are God's agents.

While I like the idea that we are created in the image of God, and believe strongly that we return the favor through our many religions, I am not comfortable that we are somehow alien to this planet. I worry that the notion that earth isn't our true home gives rise to exploitation of the earth rather than stewardship as well as the notion that we are going home after a time here on earth, so it really doesn't matter how we treat the place. In effect, we act like renters rather than owners. Even worse, we act like renters who don't seem to care about getting our security deposit back when we move on. If you've ever owned rental property, as my parents and in-laws did, you know what I'm talking about.

I feel at home here on earth, and find great meaning in the Bible's linkage of earthling and earth (*adam* and *adamah* in the original Hebrew) found in Genesis' second story of human creation:

> These are the generations of the heavens and
> the earth when they were created. In the day
> that the Eternal God made the earth and
> the heavens, when no plant of the field was
> yet in the earth and no herb of the field had
> yet sprung up—for the Eternal God had not
> caused it to rain upon the earth, and there was
> no one to till the ground; but a stream would
> rise from the earth, and water the whole face
> of the ground—then the Eternal God formed
> the groundling from the dust of the ground,
> and breathed into his nostrils the breath of
> life; and the groundling became a living being.
> (Genesis 2:4–7, NRSV, adapted)

What I like about Genesis 1 is that men and
women are created at the same time. What I don't like
is that they seem alien to the earth. What I don't like
about Genesis 2 is that women are created after men
(Genesis 2:22). What I like is that humans have their
origins in the *humus*, the earth. If God had asked me
for editorial advice, I would have told one story:

> Then God said to the animals just formed, "Let
> us make humankind in our image, according

to our likeness—a little bit you, a little bit Me;
and let them watch over this world and protect
it from malls and politicians." So God gathered
together earth of all colors and created
earthlings, women and men, of every hue. And
God said to them, "You are the earth become
conscious. Be kind to one another and to all
life. And try not to divide yourselves by tribe
or religion or nation states. And if you do,
don't invent gunpowder. And if you do, don't
invent nuclear weapons. And if you do, don't
come crying to Me for help."

Clearly God didn't ask for my help in writing the
Bible, but by giving us a choice of creation stories,
God lets us decide to tell one that reminds us that this
planet is home. We are thinking dust, talking dirt, and
how cool is that!?!

The philosopher Alan Watts tells a parable of aliens
coming to visit planet earth when it was pretty much
just a rock. They flew by, took a couple of notes, and
dismissed the place as irrelevant. A second team of
aliens returns millions of years later to find this rock
teeming with creative life. They are astounded by this
fact and humbled by their own inability to predict it.

Of course, if Watts were writing today, his aliens would call home and order an invasion of planet earth, leading to an all-out war that would leave both peoples dying for a sequel. But he wrote in the sixties, which, if you weren't fighting in the jungles of Vietnam or on the streets of Selma, was a kinder and gentler time. Anyway, for Watts, and for me, the planet earth peoples the way an apple tree apples. You can attribute the peopling of earth to God or Nature, and you can, as the Hindu Vedantists in India do, equate the two with nature being an expression of God the way waves are expressions of the ocean.

What I like about this story is that it makes us at home on and responsible for the well-being of planet earth. Which leads me back to Play-Doh. You can do this exercise by purchasing some Play-Doh or making your own play dough. If you choose the latter, here's a recipe I adapted from www.instructables.com/id/How-to-Make-Playdough-Play-doh/:

> You'll need 2 cups of flour, 2 cups of warm water, 1 cup of salt, 2 tablespoons of vegetable oil, 1 teaspoon of cream, and some food coloring. Putting the food coloring aside, mix all the other ingredients together and stir over

a low heat. The dough will thicken up and
eventually coalesce in the center of the pot.
When it does, remove from the heat and let
the mess cool enough for you to work with.
Knead the dough until it becomes silky, and
then divide it into balls. Poke a hole in each
ball and add some food coloring. Avoid getting
the dye on your hands or counter. Knead the
dough some more until the balls are the colors
of your choice. You can deepen the colors by
adding more dye.

Now you are ready to play with the dough. This
stuff is edible, so it's safe for your kids. It is highly salty
though, so chances are they won't eat a second help-
ing, but your dog might. Keep the play dough away
from Fido.

Roll the dough balls into a big ball. This
is earth. With the help of your kids, pull
mountains, rivers, trees, and even people up
from the earth. Don't pull them off and then
stick them back on—that's not how things
happened. The earth grew people the way a
peach tree grows peaches: organically. Fill

planet play dough with as much life as you can imagine, and talk to your kids about how people grow on the tree of life like buds grow on a branch.

This is the story you are telling your children:

Your precious tube is part of a larger system called planet earth, which itself is part of an even larger system called the universe. The earth grew you the same way it grows trees and bumblebees and fireflies. And for the same reason: life is always experimenting with ways to be alive. You are one of those ways.

Nothing separates you from the rest of life. We are all part of the body of the whole universe. But we have something that some parts of life don't have and something that some other parts do have but not as much as we have. And that is the ability to know the story and the moral of the story.

Dogs and cats are cute and smart and precious like you, but they don't know the whole story. The more you know of the story, the more responsible you are for caring for life.

> And since you know the whole story, you are
> responsible for caring for the whole of life.

This is where you insert your values about respecting life, living lightly, etc. This is where you might teach your children (and yourself) to garden, compost, recycle, and help the ASPCA rescue and care for animals. The specifics are up to you. Different people have different values. But the story is universal. To help with this you might take a look at Todd Parr's *The EARTH Book*, Molly Bang's *Common Ground: The Water, Earth, and Air We Share*, and Lois Ehlert's *Growing Vegetable Soup*, and *Planting a Rainbow*.

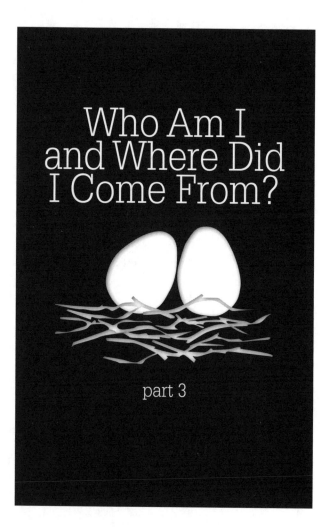

Who Am I and Where Did I Come From?

part 3

You Are God.

WE STARTED WITH the story, *You Are a Tube.* Then we expanded that to *You Are the World.* Now we are going to push things a bit further: *You Are God.* This is a tough story, and you may not want to tell it. You may not even believe it, and if you don't believe it you should definitely not tell it.

Only tell your kids stories you believe, though you need not believe them literally. There is a huge difference between truth and literal fact. A story can have no facts in it at all, and still be true. When Jesus told the story of the Good Samaritan (Luke 10:25–37), no one interrupted him to ask, "Excuse me, Rabbi Jesus, what was the name of the mugged guy and the Samaritan? I know a Samaritan and I wonder if it is the same guy. He seems nice and all."

People knew Jesus was telling a story, a parable. He was speaking truth, but not using literal facts to do so. Jesus and other great teachers always use story and metaphor. When Jesus said, "Let the dead bury the dead" (Luke 9:60), no one thought he was talking about zombies. It was a metaphor.

Telling stories to your children is not telling them things you don't believe and that they will have to unlearn and outgrow; it is sharing those things you believe most deeply in a way that speaks to them at their level of understanding. The kinds of stories I am advocating in this *Guide* are stories you want your children to grow into rather than out of.

When my son was just learning to talk, I got him to parrot the phrase "God is the root of all things," in response to the question *Who is God?* I was in rabbinical school and God was on the mind of many of my friends, and getting Aaron to say this was cute, albeit heretical even in a Reform seminary. Few of my friends took God seriously enough to worry about an apostate toddler, so his response remained on the level of cute.

If I were turning my child into a religious parrot today, I would teach a different theology. I am no longer content with God as the root of all things; for me, God is root, branch, leaf, earth, sky, etc. To be blunt: God is the Source and Substance of all reality. There is nothing that isn't God.

If it is true that God is everything, then God is you as well. This is what it means to be infinite, and many people who believe in God believe that God is infinite. Well, if God is infinite, there can't be anything outside of God. If there were something outside of God, that something would be other than God, and that would mean that God isn't infinite. Lots of people believe in finite Gods—Gods who live somewhere in particular rather than everywhere in general—but I am not one of them.

Of course if you believe God is everything and anything that transcends everything if there is such a thing, you don't really need to use the word "God" at all. So drop it if you like. You can speak of Nature, or Reality, or the Universe, or Tao, or Godhead, or Brahman, or Ayn Sof (the Unending), or any number of verbal stand-ins for "everything that was, is, and will ever be."

I still use the word "God" and do so for two reasons. First, it lets me answer "yes" when someone asks me if I believe in God. Second, it allows me to tweak the idea of God when I then explain what I mean by God.

The truth is, however, that I don't *believe* in God; I know God. We believe in that which we cannot know or prove. I don't say, "I believe I have a sister," I know I have a sister. I might not know where she is at the moment, and I might say, "I believe my sister is at work," because I cannot be certain that she is at work, but I know she exists. In the same way, I don't *believe* in God, I know God. God is reality: the stuff—both material and immaterial—that I encounter each and every moment.

Is this just semantics? Of course it is. Semantics is all we've got. We live in a world of words. In the first chapter of Genesis we are told that God spoke the universe into existence, and in the first chapter of the Gospel According to John we are told that "in the beginning was the word, and the word was with God, and the word was God" (John 1:1). A few verses later we are told "the word became flesh" (John 1:14). In my English translation of the Greek Gospel According to John, the word "word" is capitalized to suggest that it is more than a mere word. But the original Greek had no capital letters, so this is really the gloss of an editor trying to make a theological point out of a grammatical vaguery.

We live in a world of words. In Hebrew, the words "word" and "thing" are comprised of the same three consonants: *d–v–r*. So while it is true that I cannot build a tree house in the word "tree," I can build a tree and a tree house in your mind simply by saying "tree" and "tree house."

You could even say that words are a way we humans get to know the world. Again, look at Genesis. The first thing that the earthling does is name the animals as God creates them. Remember, the Hebrew word *adam* means earthling, not man, and comes from the Hebrew word *adamah*/earth, just as the word *human* comes from *humus*, earth (not to be confused with *hummus* which is a chickpea paste you eat with pita bread).

> Eternal God formed from the ground every
> animal of the field and every bird of the air,
> and brought them to the earthling to be
> named; and whatever the earthling called each
> living creature, that was its name. (Genesis
> 2:19 NRSV, adapted)

59

Bob Dylan wrote a wonderful song about this in his 1990 album *Slow Train Coming*, and, with illustrator Jim Arnosky, turned it into a children's book, *Man Gave Names to All the Animals* (clearly, Dylan's Hebrew wasn't that good).

Genesis seems to suggest that God didn't have names for the birds or animals and left the naming up to *adam*, the earthling. We are still at it. We name things as a way of becoming familiar with them. Naming something removes the element of the unknown that for us humans often carries a bit of fear. Naming is an act of overcoming fear and befriending whatever feels like "other."

So I choose to name reality "God" for the same reason I choose to name my dog "Murphy:" it's shorthand. I could refer to her as my "hybrid canine, crossbred from a Golden Retriever and a Poodle, who is smart and highly social and loves to fetch sticks, balls, and Frisbees," but saying, "Sit, hybrid canine, crossbred from a Golden Retriever and a Poodle, who is smart and highly social, and loves to fetch sticks, balls, and Frisbees, sit" is much more difficult than saying, "Sit, Murphy, sit." So I opt for "Murphy."

You can use the word "God" any way you wish, or choose not to use it at all, but however you understand reality, and whatever you call reality, you are most likely going to pass this on to your children through stories. So what stories do you tell about God/Reality?

A reporter once asked Albert Einstein, "What do you think is the most important question facing humanity today?" Einstein replied,

> I think the most important question facing humanity is, *Is the universe a friendly place?* This is the first and most basic question all people must answer for themselves.
>
> For if we decide that the universe is an unfriendly place, then we will use our technology, our scientific discoveries and our natural resources to achieve safety and power by creating bigger walls to keep out the unfriendliness and bigger weapons to destroy all that which is unfriendly, and I believe that we are getting to a place where technology is powerful enough that we may either completely isolate or destroy ourselves as well in this process.
>
> If we decide that the universe is neither friendly nor unfriendly and that God is essentially playing dice with the universe, then

61

we are simply victims to the random toss of the dice and our lives have no real purpose or meaning.

But if we decide that the universe is a friendly place, then we will use our technology, our scientific discoveries and our natural resources to create tools and models for understanding that universe. Because power and safety will come through understanding its workings and its motives.

I would modify Einstein's reply this way: not *Is the universe friendly*, but *Does the universe allow for friendship?* The universe is too vast and too wild to be friendly the way most of us use the term. But it certainly allows for friendship, and we may conclude that befriending life is a better strategy than fearing it.

You could say the same thing about God. Is your God friendly or not?

I know lots of people who, taking Jesus as God, say that Jesus is more than just friendly, he is their eternal best friend. The fact that they believe their BFF is going to condemn me and my family and lots of my friends to eternal torment in hell doesn't make me any less a believer in friendship, but it does make me a bit hesitant about hanging out with their Jesus.

I wouldn't say my God, Reality, is friendly, exactly. I have seen too many *NOVA* episodes about exploding stars and the end of the earth to say that. But I do believe God makes room for friendship. After all, God/Reality births a glorious universe filled with wondrous forces that are just perfectly suited to give birth to and sustain human life, and the best way to do that seems to be by befriending one another and the species with whom we share the planet. God isn't anti-friendly; God simply transcends what you and I might consider friendly when it comes to a human friend.

So there is no question that God is greater than friendship, but that doesn't mean that God doesn't also include friendship. God is friendly, in that God, Reality, makes life, and human life in particular, possible.

Following Einstein's thinking, if God is unfriendly, we would have to use all our resources to control God. This may be the origin of sacrificial religions: something has to die or God is going to kill us. That something may be a child, an animal, or even God's Son, but without death to placate God, we humans are in for a world of hurt.

This kind of religion makes us very anxious: What if we say the wrong words, perform the wrong ritual or the right ritual in the wrong way or at the wrong time—then what? Leviticus 10 tells us what. When Aaron's two sons, Nadab and Abihu, offered an unrequired fire sacrifice to God, God responded by burning them to a crisp (Leviticus 10:1–3).

This isn't the kind of God I know or the kind of story I want to tell my kids. But lots of us do tell such stories. Lots of kids are scared to death of God, and lots of kids are scared to death of life. My experience suggests that scared kids grow up to be scary adults.

I teach Bible at Middle Tennessee State University (MTSU). Bible study at a secular college is not the same as Bible Study at a church or synagogue. We challenge everything the church or synagogue may take as true. We begin with the assumption that the Bible is a human document, an artifact of a given time and place reflecting the beliefs and biases of its authors. Churches and synagogue Bible Study often begins with the assumption that the Bible is written by or, at the very least, inspired by God, a being whose very existence is questioned in the academy.

Both assumptions have value, and I can teach Bible

in both settings. But when I teach in the university, I am careful not to begin with the assumption of the synagogue or church.

A few years ago I noticed that one young woman in my Bible class at MTSU concluded each class with some muttering under her breath. She always sat in the first row, and while I could not discern what she was saying, it was clear that she was saying something, maybe even the same thing, at the end of every class session. After a while I asked her what she was saying.

"I'm praying," she said. "I pray to God saying, 'Please don't take me tonight; I don't know what I believe.'" When I asked her explain the meaning of her prayer, she told me that she believed that if she died with less than perfect faith, God would send her soul to burn in hell for all eternity. Since my teachings during class caused her to reconsider what she was taught in Sunday school, she feared dying on Tuesday or Thursday nights when the ideas I presented were still challenging her.

I did my best to suggest that God was too loving to punish her for giving me the courtesy of her attention during class and that if there was a sin involved, it would be mine not hers, but she would have none of it. "No," she said, "it's safer if I just keep praying." Maybe so. Clearly the story of a damning God had a deep hold on her, and while I commend her courage to study Bible at a secular university, I am saddened by the fear she was fed that haunted her twice-weekly.

So, *Who are you?* You are the self-consciousness of life. You are the universe capable of saying, "I am the universe."

And *Where did you come from?* You grew from the universe the same way an apple grows from an apple tree.

I would take this a bit further and say, "You are a part of God the way a wave is a part of the ocean. Everything is a part of God, and nothing is apart from God. Everything is in God, and God is in everything, and if you learn to look closely enough, you will discover that God is all there is. And, as we shall see, learning to look closely and see God is why you are here.

There Is Nowhere to Go.

WHAT HAPPENS when I die? That is really what we are asking when we ask, *Where am I going?* Your answer to *Where am I going?* depends on your answer to *Where did I come from?* There are basically four stories you can tell your children regarding the afterlife:

1. *Winners and Losers*: A Story of Heaven and Hell

2. *I'll Be Back*: A Story of Reincarnation

3. *Here We Go Again*: A Story of Recycling

4. *When You're Dead You're Dead*: A Story of the End of the Story

Which story you tell is highly personal; in my experience, it's the most personal story you will ever tell. In fact, the story you tell about what happens after you die may reveal more about you than any other story you tell. Each of these stories comes in dozens of variations, and I won't pretend to do them all justice. Rather, I will highlight the core message of each category of story and the values I think it fosters.

WINNERS AND LOSERS

Winners and Losers is a story about God's justice, and offers children a sense that the world is a fair place where the good are rewarded and the wicked are punished. God likes good people and dislikes bad people. The people God likes go to heaven, the people God doesn't like go to hell. Heaven is a place of peace and love. Hell is a place of endless suffering, torment, and horror. Nobody wants to go to hell, but lots of people refuse to do what it takes to get into heaven. God doesn't want people to go to hell, but God will only let those people into heaven who do what is necessary to get into heaven. Everyone else goes to hell. God isn't happy about this, but it is our choice.

What it takes to get into heaven differs among different people. Since *Winners and Losers* is a story generally told by Jews, Christians, and Muslims, we will stick to the basic teachings of these three communities, admitting from the first that these religions are not monolithic and not all adherents believe the same things. Judaism, for example, says that anyone whose good deeds outweigh her bad deeds goes to heaven. Christianity, for the most part, focuses on the sincerity of one's belief in Jesus Christ—limiting heaven to true believers rather than good behavers, though there is an assumption that true believers would also be good behavers. And Islam seems to mix the two: good believers (who would also be good behavers) and good behavers (who may not be good believers) both get into heaven.

I suspect, however, that the real power of *Winners and Losers* isn't about winning, as much as it is about not losing. That is to say, some of us who tell the *Winners and Losers* story are comforted not by winners going to heaven but by losers going to hell. There is, for some people, something comforting about knowing that people they don't like are being tortured in hell for all eternity.

I once attended a clergy panel discussion on various Christian traditions. During the Q & A someone asked about the fate of nonChristians after they die. I was the only person in the room openly identified as a nonChristian, and the panelists looked in my direction, hesitant to respond out of respect for my feelings. As the pressure mounted for some reply, the Lutheran pastor smiled at me and said, "Nothing personal, Rabbi, but you will burn in hell for all eternity."

Nothing personal? It seemed personal to me, seeing as it would be me who would be burning. But, since I don't tell this story or put much stock in it, I wasn't really concerned.

During the coffee break that followed this comment on my fate, three other pastors rushed over to assure me that the Lutheran pastor's position, while valid, was not the only Christian position. He is, they told me, an Eternalist, one who believes that torture of the damned is eternal. They, however, were Annihilationists. While it is true I will be condemned to burn in hell, after a few thousand years the fires of hell will at last consume my soul, and I will cease to exist. I will be annihilated, and with that annihilation, my pain and suffering will come to an end.

I agreed with my colleagues that the Annihilationist position is more comforting than the Eternalist position, but added that on a scale from one to ten, they both suck. Why, I asked, would a God of love condemn anyone to hell, let alone a decent person who simply believed in a faith other than Protestant Christianity?

"God is like a parent, and parents do punish their children. It's for their own good."

"Sure," I said, "but any parent who punishes his or her child with eternal torture would be arrested and sent to prison. Shouldn't God be better than a child molester? And while we are on the subject of child abuse, why is it that God needs the murder of His Son Jesus before He can forgive people for the sin of Adam and Eve? I would think an all-powerful, all-loving God could forgive people without killing anyone, let alone His Son."

The pastors looked at one another, then at me, and then back to one another, and then again at me. They smiled, and drifted off. Clearly I was going to hell. And I suspect they were wondering if the Eternalist position wasn't the preferred option after all.

Please don't imagine that all Christians believe that all nonChristians are going to hell. Many Catholic priests tell me, for example, that as I die Jesus will come to me and offer me a chance at salvation by accepting Him as my Lord and Savior. I have no doubt that if this happens I will opt for Jesus and Heaven over hanging out with my people in hell, but that says more about me and my aversion to extreme heat and torture than it does about the Jewish religion. And there are many liberal Christian denominations that don't believe in hell, or, even if they do, don't imagine that good people go there, even if they don't believe in Jesus.

Anyway, the message of *Winners and Losers* isn't so much about who wins and who loses as it is about a God who isn't all that friendly. In fact, *Winners and Losers* can make people very anxious. They never seem secure in winning and therefore worry a lot about losing. If you choose to tell this story to your kids, try and do so in a way that doesn't scare them too much, or make them afraid to hang out with other kids who, according to your version of *Winners and Losers*, are clearly losers.

I'LL BE BACK

People who believe in reincarnation tell the *I'll Be Back* story, and most of these are Hindus and Buddhists, though a growing number of Americans who practice yoga and are in the "spiritual but not religious" camp tell it as well. Like *Winners and Losers*, *I'll Be Back* is a story about justice: you reap what you sow. Those who do good in this life get a better next life; those who do badly in this life get a worse next life. There is more to reincarnation than this, but that is the gist of how most people seem to understand it.

The theory behind reincarnation is *karma*. The word is Sanskrit for "action" and means that every action has a consequence. When you see the wicked prosper, it isn't that crime pays, but that they are reaping the reward of some good deed they did in the past. When you see the good suffer, it isn't that God is malicious, but that they are paying the price for some evil they did in the past. There is no statute of limitations with regard to karma.

Karma should not be confused with fate or destiny. Fate and destiny imply that your life is scripted for you before you were born, and you had nothing to do with the writing of this script. Calvinists who believe that God predetermines who will go to heaven and who will go to hell before they are ever born, believe in fate and destiny but not karma. You create your own karma; God has nothing to do with it. And you will be forced to deal with the karmic consequences of your actions whether God exists or not. Karma, like gravity, is a force of nature.

Some people use karma to promote compassion, and some use it to excuse the opposite. Knowing that we are all working out our karmic consequences, we can have compassion for those who suffer, since they are paying a debt accrued in a past life that may have been lived very differently than the current life in which the suffering is happening. Karma determines the situations in which we find ourselves, not our responses to those situations. So whether you are suffering or celebrating, your actions in this moment will set in motion forces that will create the condition for future moments. If you take your suffering out on others, you are creating more negative karma for yourself. If, on the other hand, you use your suffering to soften your heart and reach out to do more good in the world, you are creating good karma that will ripen into positive situations in the future.

On the other hand, there are those who look at the suffering of others and say, "Well, that's their karma, and I have nothing to do with it." This is a misuse of karma. When you do nothing to feed the hungry, house the homeless, and clothe the naked, you are not simply leaving them to their bad karma; you are generating bad karma for yourself. It was your karma to be confronted with people in need. How you handle this confrontation will generate new karma and determine your future either in this life and some other.

Like *Winners and Losers*, *I'll Be Back* comes in lots of variations. If you are going to tell this story, take care to do so in a manner that promotes compassion rather than hardheartedness.

HERE WE GO AGAIN

This is my story. It is similar to *I'll Be Back* but different in a way that is crucial as well. *I'll Be Back* posits a self or soul that puts on and takes off lives the way you might put on and take off jackets. The lives and jackets may differ from one another, but the you that wears them is the same. This is closer to the Hindu and New Age versions of *I'll Be Back* than to some Buddhist versions where there is no person who reincarnates, but rather impersonal energies that converge to produce a person.

Here We Go Again agrees that life doesn't end with death, but doesn't posit a *you* that travels from life to life creating karma and reaping its rewards. In the *Here We Go Again* story, as I tell it, you are a temporary expression of God the way a wave is a temporary expression of the ocean. No wave ever comes back once it returns to the ocean, but the ocean itself continually waves. So too with *Here We Go Again*: *Rami* is the only Rami that will ever be, but *Rami* is a manifestation of God, and when I die I will simply become what I already am—God—and God will continue to manifest lives, just not my life.

Think of it this way:

> Imagine you are standing on a rocky seashore on the California coast. And imagine that the waves you see rolling in from the Pacific toward the rocks are self-aware the way we humans are self-aware. Imagine also that they can talk and that you can hear and understand what they are saying. Like humans do among themselves, these waves will use their self-awareness to compare themselves with other waves. Some are wider, some thinner; some are taller, some shorter. After a while you hear them starting to panic: "Where did Janice go? She was just ahead of us by those rocks and now she's gone. Where is she?"

Soon it will become painfully obvious
to these waves that when they hit the rocks
something horrible happens—they shatter and
die. But maybe not. Maybe there is life after
beach. Some waves argue that it only looks
like Janice is gone, when in fact she is waving
in a shoreless sea beyond the rocks. Others
argue that she has been placed back in the
ocean, but far behind them where she can't be
seen. Others have other ideas, and they argue
passionately, even vehemently, in favor of their
respective ideas, especially as they get closer to
the rocks.

You are hearing all this, and you can't
help but laugh. Your heart goes out to these
panicking waves, but you know they will be
fine. All that happens when they hit the rocks
is that they lose their shape. They aren't really
other than the ocean, and they will simply
return to the ocean where waving continues,
though no particular wave is ever repeated.
You call out to them to comfort them, but
while you can understand them, they cannot
understand you. You feel their pain, and

find comfort in knowing that they worry for nothing.

I've known lots of Janices and lots of worried waves. I'm usually the guy on the beach. This is how I teach this story to children:

> Give your child a length of rope about eight inches long. Have her tie a knot in the rope, and then ask her to describe the knot: How big is it? How tight or loose is it? That kind of thing. Once your child has described the knot, ask about the relationship between knot and rope. Is the knot other than the rope? Could the knot exist without rope?
>
> Your child will realize that the knot is simply an expression of the rope—the rope in a certain shape—and not something other than the rope.
>
> Now let's name the knot. If there has been a death in your family—a grandparent, a pet, etc.—name the knot after the deceased. When I do this exercise with kids, I name my knot Fanny after my mom's mom.

Having named the first knot, have your child tie a second knot on the rope. Give this knot your child's name. Compare the two knots. They are not the same. One is a bit older than the other; one may be a bit tighter or looser than the other; one is in one place on the rope, the other in another place. And yet they are both the same rope and nothing other than the rope.

Now talk about the rope as God, Reality, or Nature. Imagine that the rope is all there is, and everything is a knot of the rope. You are teaching that God, Reality, and Nature manifest in many forms, each unique and distinct from the others, yet none other than or separate from God, Reality, or Nature itself.

This is a story about death, so it is time to mark the passing of our first knot, Fanny, in my case. Untie the original knot; Fanny has died. But where did she go? Sure, her shape is gone, but is the rope any more or less? Is the rope that was Fanny missing? Is the Rami knot any less connected to Fanny now that the knot we called Fanny is gone?

To the extent we love and cherish the knot—Fanny—we miss her. We miss her shape, her smell, her stories, and her love. Everything that we remember about her is gone, but the rope that she was still is. And because it still is, the connection with Fanny isn't broken.

Now tie a third knot in the rope. This isn't Fanny (that would be the story *I'll Be Back*); there is no way to replicate the Fanny knot perfectly. It is simply another knot, for the rope keeps knotting the way an ocean keeps waving.

The reason I love this story is that it leads me to an understanding of myself and others that honors our differences without imagining them to be permanent. It allows me to be the precious tube I am, while showing me that I am so much more: I am both knot and rope, wave and ocean, part and whole. This allows your children to honor their uniqueness without becoming attached to it.

Why not be attached? Because people change and ultimately die. Because your children will change and ultimately die. If they are attached to who they were, they may reject who they have become. If they limit their understanding of self to the temporary knot or wave, they miss the greater truth that they are the rope and ocean. They are God—just not all of God. And so is everything else.

WHEN YOU'RE DEAD, YOU'RE DEAD

This is the story you tell if you believe that life ends with death. When someone dies, all connection with him or her dies as well. And while we can remember those we love who have died, we cannot in any way feel a real connection with them outside of memory.

The power of *When You're Dead, You're Dead* is that it highlights the preciousness of life. This is your one chance at life, and you had best make the most of it. What that most is depends on other stories you tell your children.

You may tell them that making the most means owning the most, or loving the most, or doing the most, or being the most famous. Or you may tell them that making the most means being true to yourself: your sense of right and wrong, your unique gifts, your deepest desires.

One of the best stories for telling *When You're*

Dead, You're Dead is Humpty Dumpty. Each of us is Humpty Dumpty. We are sitting on a wall—life—and in time and perhaps for no obvious reason we will have a great fall—death. And no matter what all the king's horses and all the king's men try to do, there is no way they can put Humpty Dumpty together again. The point of your life on the wall is to do as much as you can because eventually you will fall and you will never come back.

My favorite version of *When You're Dead, You're Dead* is a Zen story about a man and a strawberry.

> Once upon a time a village was threatened by a people-eating tiger. The villagers hoped to kill the tiger and tried to trap it. They dug a deep pit and put sharpened bamboo poles at the bottom of it. They covered the top of the pit with grass so the tiger wouldn't notice the pit. When the tiger walked on the grass, he would fall into the pit and be killed on the bamboo spikes. The village would be saved.
>
> Having dug and covered the pit, the villagers went home to wait. Unfortunately, a man from a different village, unaware of the tiger or the plan to kill him, came to visit

friends in this village. Not noticing the trap, the man stepped on the grass and fell into the pit. He surely would have died, but as he fell, he saw a vine hanging down the side of the pit, and grabbed it, stopping his fall. All he had to do was climb out of the pit using the vine as a ladder.

As he began to climb out of the pit, the tiger came by, and peering into the pit saw the man whom he decided would make a delightful meal. The man stopped climbing. If he climbed out, the tiger would eat him. If he let go the spikes would kill him. So he waited, certain that if he waited long enough the tiger would go away.

Just then, as he was clinging to the vine waiting for the tiger to leave, a mole poked his head out of the side of the pit and began chewing on the vine. It tasted good, and the mole was going to eat all the way through the vine, snapping it in two and sending the man to his death. There was nothing he could do to save himself. If he scampered up the vine and out of the pit, the tiger would eat him. If he waited until the vine snapped, the spikes would kill him.

It was then that the man noticed a large strawberry growing on the vine right by his hand. He plucked the strawberry and popped it into his mouth. "Oh my!" the man said aloud, "That is the best strawberry I have ever tasted!"

Death isn't the enemy of life; it makes living all the more precious.

You can tell this story even if you don't believe in the *When You're Dead, You're Dead* story. Even if you believe, as I do, in the *Here We Go Again* story, the tale of the man and the strawberry still makes sense. After all, when the knot is gone, it is gone forever; when the wave is shattered, it is never put back together again. Knowing that the rope still knots and the ocean still waves doesn't make any one knot or wave any less special. This life is the only one you will have, though living goes on regardless. So make the most of it. See each moment as precious, every strawberry as luscious. When you measure life in time, every minute counts.

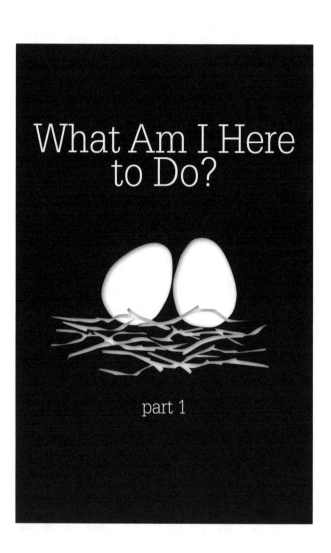

What Am I Here to Do?

part 1

CHAPTER **FIVE**

To Open Your Heart, Stretch Out Your Hand, Broaden Your Mind.

STORIES THAT ANSWER the question *What Am I Here to Do?* are called heart stories. They are called heart stories because they either open or close your heart. When your heart opens, compassion arises. When compassion arises, you naturally reach out to be of service to others. And when you are of service to others, you get to know them and expand your mind.

Another way to say this is that there are only two kinds of heart stories: those that engender love and those that engender fear. Don't mistake love for romance or fear for being scared. There is nothing wrong with either, but the love I'm talking about makes you curious about life and courageous when living it, while the fear I'm talking about constricts the heart and alienates you from life.

Many years ago a friend told me of an incident while she was in college. It was her freshman year and she was sharing a dorm room with a delightful and devoted Christian woman. My friend is Jewish. The two young women got along wonderfully, and as their friendship grew, the Christian roommate felt comfortable enough to ask a very personal question of her Jewish friend: "Would you show me your horns?"

"My what?"

"Your horns. You know . . . You're Jewish, and Jews have horns, so . . . You keep them covered up under your hair, and I just thought, well, we're such good friends and all, that you wouldn't mind showing me your horns."

My friend had no idea what her roommate was talking about. She had never heard the story that Jews have horns. The more she asked her friend about it, the more horrified she became. Jews have horns, her friend said, because they are the children of Satan, and Satan, their father, has horns.

"Is this really what you think? That my father is Satan? That Jews are the devil's children? Here, look for yourself! See if I have horns! What a stupid thing to believe!"

Their friendship survived this encounter, and thankfully her roommate's belief in Jews with horns did not.

One can trace the story that Jews have horns to Exodus 34:29. When Moses came down from Mount Sinai after speaking with God, his face shone with beams (*karan* in Hebrew) of light. In the fifth century, St. Jerome mistook *karan*, beam, for *keren*, horn, and wrote his Latin translation of the Hebrew Bible accordingly. A thousand years later, Michelangelo sculpted Moses with two strange bumps on his head—whether he meant them to be beams of light or horns we don't know—and five centuries after that my friend's roommate took that to mean all Jews have horns.

My friend's roommate assumed Jewish horns linked them to Satan because, as she explained, she was taught in church that Jews were the devil's children (John 8:44). Given that Satan has horns, it is only logical that Jews would have horns also. The story this young woman was told demonized Jews. Had these two young women not been assigned the same dorm room, and had they not been the kind of people who were curious about differences rather than frightened of them, who knows how many more generations of this young Christian woman's family would have been brought up to believe Jews bear the horns of their satanic father?

When I talk about stories that perpetuate fear, this is the kind of story I have in mind. We all carry these "othering" stories. They may be about Jews, African Americans, Mexican Americans, Muslims, Christians, homosexuals, women, or any number of people we might fear. We tell othering stories to keep the other at bay.

As I was growing up, I was told stories about Christians that carried a very simple moral: every Christian is a closet anti-Semite—watch out! Don't trust them. No matter what they say, they secretly hate you for being God's Chosen People.

Othering stories are common in the Hebrew Bible. NonJews are dangerous. They worship false gods and will entice you to do the same. In the Book of Deuteronomy, God tells the Israelites that when they go to war against gentiles outside the Promised Land they should first offer terms of surrender. If the gentiles do surrender, the Jews should take them as slaves. If they don't surrender, the Jews were to slaughter all the men, and, if they like, take the women and children as plunder along with the cattle and gold (Deuteronomy 20:10–16).

With regard to gentiles in the Promised Land, "you must not let anything that breathes remain alive . . . so that they may not teach you to do all the abhorrent things that they do for their gods, and you thus sin against the Eternal your God" (Deuteronomy 20:16–18, NRSV, adapted). Why the Israelites can resist the theological wiles of those gentile women outside the Promised Land but not those inside the Promised Land isn't explained. But they can't, so to be safe they had better murder them all.

While you might prefer Jesus' "the Jews are Satan spawn" to God's "slaughter the gentiles in the Promised Land," the truth is they both led to genocide. All "othering" stories do.

So what kind of stories are you going to tell your kids? Are they Chosen, while everyone else comes up with the silver medal at best? Are they saved, while billions of others are going to burn for all eternity in hell? Are they true believers sworn to defend the faith by slaughtering the infidels? Are they of a higher caste, while others are lower or perhaps so low as to be beneath caste and hence untouchable? Should they fear black people, white people, Puerto Ricans? These are all constricting, fear-based stories we may have been told and may repeat to our children without realizing it. Stories told long enough cease to be stories and become facts.

People aren't born to fear other people based on race, color, religion, ethnicity, gender, or sexual preference. We have to be taught to do this, and we are taught through the stories we are told. That's why we try and tell these stories to our children early—before they can think about them and perhaps challenge them. We tell our stories early so that they can take root and influence our children's behavior subconsciously. But we aren't born with these stories; they are taught to us early by our parents and grandparents, our schools, our media, and our culture in general.

Take the othering of fat people. Can you recall a positive image of a fat person shown on television or in the movies? From Bill Cosby's *Fat Albert* to CBS' *Mike and Molly*, fat people are funny because they are fat. Or watch the news: fat people are stupid, lazy, poor, and responsible for much of the health crisis faced by the United States.

Were you born with an innate dislike for fat people? Or did you learn this growing up? And if you are fat, do you hate yourself for being fat? I spent much of my youth in fat camps and all of my life fighting my weight. I can tell you the only thing fat kids hated more than even fatter kids was themselves. You aren't born hating yourself. You learn that.

This is true of all othering stories, even ones in which the other is yourself. You have to hear them over and over and over again until they are true simply because they are ubiquitous.

So, again, what kinds of stories are you telling yourself and your children? Do they expand or contract the heart?

One of my favorite sources for stories is the television series *Star Trek* in all its permutations. The fourteenth episode of the third season of the original series was called "Let That Be Your Last Battlefield." The Enterprise picks up two men, Lokai and Bele. Each man is black on one side and white on the other, though each differs as to which side is black and which is white. This difference is enough to plunge their two peoples into never-ending war. As the episode closes, we discover that this war has resulted in the annihilation of both peoples: Lokai and Bele may be the last of their respective peoples. This fact only fuels their hatred of one another, with each blaming the other for the war. The two beings return to their desolate planet to continue the war between them.

This is a quintessential story of heart closing. Lokai and Bele cannot make peace even when they are the last of their respective peoples.

A *Star Trek* example of a heart-opening story comes from *Star Trek: The Next Generation*, season five, episode two, "Darmok."

The Enterprise contacts a Tamarian ship orbiting around the planet El-Adrei. The Tamarian language is linked to its mythology, and without an understanding of that mythology, Captain Picard and the Enterprise crew cannot communicate with the Tamarians. Out of frustration, Dathon, the Tamarian captain, transports himself and Picard to the planet's surface where he hopes they can live out the central Tamarian story, "Darmok and Jalad at Tanagra," where two warriors are forced to collaborate to defeat a monster, and in so doing become friends.

In their attempt to defeat the monster on El-Adrei,

Dathon is mortally wounded. Captain Picard tries to save Dathon's life and, as he does, it slowly dawns on him what Dathon was trying to communicate—not enmity, but potential friendship. The two captains achieve that friendship just before Dathon dies.

The two stories have much in common. Each pits two people or peoples against one another in mortal combat, and each ends in death. But the difference between them is huge. Lokai and Bele would rather kill one another than come to understand one another. Picard and Dathon break through the fear of difference and find common ground through mutual understanding. Lokai and Bele close their hearts; Dothan and Picard open their hearts.

To help you tell heart-expanding stories, take a look at *We're Different, We're the Same*, a Sesame Street book by Bobbi Jane Kates and illustrated by Joe Mathieu, *The Big Book for Peace*, edited by Ann Durell and Marilyn Sachs, and Ezra Jack Keats' *Louie*.

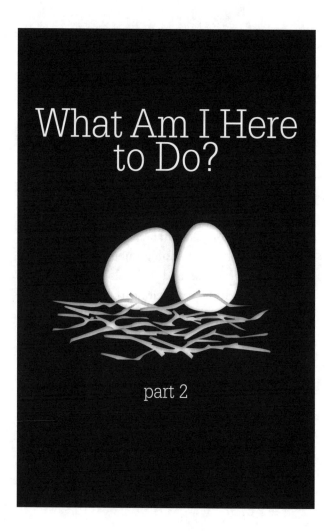

What Am I Here to Do?

part 2

How Big a Slice?
How Small a Pie?

HEART-OPENING AND heart-closing stories depend on your worldview: do you believe in a zero-sum world or a nonzero-sum world? A zero-sum worldview sees the world as a fixed pie with ever more people competing over ever-smaller slices. If you want more, others will have to get less. You can't make the pie bigger, you can only make other people's slices smaller.

A nonzero-sum worldview imagines a pie that grows, where the success of one isn't dependent upon the failure of another. Before we go into this, let me tell you what nonzero-sum is not. Nonzero-sum isn't about sameness or a one-size-fits-all policy of imposed equality. There are winners and losers in the nonzero-sum world, just as there are winners and losers in the zero-sum world. The difference is that in the zero-sum world the winners determine the losers, while in the nonzero-sum world the losers lose all by themselves.

There is a wonderful story about heaven and hell that comes in different versions, depending on which religious tradition tells it. The essence of the story is this: A great sage is about to die and asks God to show him heaven and hell. God agrees and allows the sage to peer into the depths of hell. There he sees a glorious banquet. Everyone is seated at the table which is six feet wide and infinitely long. The table is heaped with the finest foods and all are encouraged to eat as much as they wish. The only requirement is that they use their knives, forks, and spoons, each of which is also six feet long. Given the length of an arm in relation to the utensils, and hence the impossibility of feeding oneself, the feasting folks in hell are starving.

The sage is then shown the fate of those bound for heaven. Here he sees the same banquet with the same requirement. But in heaven people have learned to feed one another rather than themselves, so all are fed and none go hungry.

The suffering of hell, the suffering of the zero-sum world is not imposed by others, but by one's self.

When we overcome the selfishness of zero-sum hell, we create the joy of nonzero-sum heaven.

Nice story. But it doesn't get at the real horror of living in a zero-sum world. Here is a story that does.

Growing up, I had a friend whose parents taught him to always be the best. Not the best he could be, but the best. That meant no one could be better than him. No one could run faster, jump higher, or do better in school. If he wasn't the best, he might as well be the worst, because if only the best wins, everyone else loses.

My friend did very well for himself at school. He was a star basketball player and an honor student. He was popular, charismatic, and on the fast track to financial and maybe even political success. He applied to both Harvard and Princeton and was accepted at both. He killed himself before attending either.

He once told me, "The better I get, the better the competition gets. Eventually I am going to be with people who are all as good as me, and then I am going to lose. And when I do, my life is over and no longer worth living."

There was room for only one winner in his story,

and he knew it wasn't going to be him. Rather than face the shame of losing, he quit playing and committed suicide.

This is a quintessential zero-sum story. It is also quite extreme. I share it with you because it shows how evil zero-sum stories can be.

EVIL

Evil is real. It is not simply the absence of good, but a force in its own right. It arises when we are so consumed by the idea of winning in a zero-sum world that we are willing to do anything to achieve our goal. Winning this way means more than just having more money, or a nicer car, or a bigger house than your neighbor. Winning in this sense means having one's way and exploiting others in order to get it.

It is trite but no less instructional to note that evil is "live" spelled backwards. Evil is the antithesis of life. Where life involves you in an expanding circle of compassion arising from your growing realization that we are all one in, with, and as God (Nature, Reality, etc.), evil shrinks the circle, and leaves you fearful of others, even those closest to you. Life leads us from self to selflessness; evil leads us from self to selfishness.

More than two thousand years ago, Rabbi Hillel, an older contemporary and perhaps even a teacher of Rabbi Jesus, taught: "If I am not for myself, who will be for me? But if I am only for myself, what am I? And if not now, when?" (*Pirke Avot*, the Ethics of the Sages, 1:14) You must take care of yourself, but not yourself alone. You must rely on yourself to see to your health and welfare; no one can eat for you; no one can exercise for you, or get an education on your behalf. Having been blessed with the gift of life, you are responsible for living it. But self-reliance isn't the same as self-sufficiency.

While it is true that you must choose to eat healthfully, it is also true that the foods you consume are most likely grown by others, harvested by others, packaged by others, brought to market by others, and sold by others. And just as your body cannot live in isolation, neither can your heart, mind, or soul. So while it is up to you to optimize your life, doing so most often requires the help of others. You must be for yourself, but not only for yourself.

Being for yourself *and* for others is living optimally. Being for others, however, becomes more and more difficult when you operate in a zero-sum environment

103

where the other is seen as the competition, and your success and the success of your children depends on defeating that competition. Evil is when you set out to win regardless of the cost. Good is living in a manner that optimizes the well-being of self and others, while evil is living in a manner that optimizes the well-being of self at the expense of others.

Why am I talking about evil in a guide to parenting? Because, as the psychologist M. Scott Peck taught us decades ago, children are often the victims of evil.

> The most typical victim of evil is a child. This is to be expected because children are not only the weakest and most vulnerable members of our society but also because parents wield a power over the lives of their children that is essentially absolute . . . The child's immaturity and resulting dependency mandate its parents' possession of great power but do not negate the fact that this power, like all power, is subject to abuse of various degrees of malignancy. (M. Scott Peck, *People of the Lie*, Simon and Schuster)

Your kids come into the world story-free, and it

is the stories you tell them and the dramas you enact around them that will determine their earliest thinking about life and how best to live it. If you tell them heart-opening and nonzero-sum stories where winners win by lifting others up along the way, you are teaching them to be for self and other. If you tell them heart-closing zero-sum stories where winners win at the expense of others, you are teaching them to be for self regardless of others.

What kind of stories are you telling your children?

This is the question you must ask of yourself all the time, hence Hillel's capping phrase, *If not now, when?* If you are not now sharing stories that foster heart-opening relationships between yourself and your kids, and your kids and life, when will you do so? The answer is "never." Telling zero-sum stories is seductive, almost addictive. Such stories excuse all our selfishness and sins as necessary in a world where the pie is fixed, and to enhance the size of your slice requires you to diminish the size of everyone else's.

Because.

I WANT TO TEACH YOU a Hebrew phrase that I have found extraordinarily helpful in my quest to understand the purpose and meaning of life: *Lama? Kakha*. Unless you were raised with Hebrew, it is often hard to pronounce *kakha*. The "k" is pronounced like the "c" in "camp;" the "kh" is the sound you make when trying to clear your throat or you are preparing to spit. Luckily for us, its meaning rather than its correct pronunciation is what matters.

Lama is the Hebrew equivalent of the English word "why." *Kakha* is Hebrew for "it just is." *Lama? Kakha* means that things simply are the way they are, and asking *Why?* is often irrelevant. *Lama? Kakha* puts an end to endless questioning.

When your child continually asks why you have made the decision you did, you may become frustrated over having to explain not only your decision but your explanation. Out of that frustration, you might say, "Why? Because I say so, that's why?" This isn't *Lama? Kakha*. This is simply intimidating your child into silence. *Lama? Kakha* isn't the shutting down of questioning; it is the final answer to the question. But which question?

The question that *Lama? Kakha* answers is the existential question *Why?* Not the question, "Why can't I have a candy bar ten minutes before dinner?" but the question, "Why was I born?" or "Why is there life?" or "Why is there something rather than nothing?" or "Why did Mommy die," or "Why did Daddy leave," or "Why does sister Magen have cancer?" *Lama? Kakha* is the answer to those huge questions that do not lend themselves to reasoned answers. Some things just happen, and that is that.

I once heard a grieving mom respond patiently to her seven-year-old daughter's question, "Why did Daddy die in the car crash?" with "It wasn't his fault. Your dad was a good driver, but the other man had been drinking. He was drunk and couldn't drive and shouldn't have been driving. He lost control of his car and crossed into Daddy's lane and they crashed."

"But why?" her daughter asked again. She wasn't

asking for the cause and effect, she was asking for the spiritual answer, the answer that would bring meaning to her life experience.

You might respond to this question with a story entitled *It's God's Will* and hope that story provides an answer. But it only begs another question: "Why is it God's will?" You might tell a story of karma: that in a past life Daddy caused an accident that cost another person's life, and so Daddy had to pay for that mistake with his life. But this too leads to further questioning: "Why should my daddy pay for a mistake in this life that some other person's daddy made in another life?"

The point is, there are some questions that cannot be answered, and we shouldn't try to answer them. We have to learn to live with not-knowing. *Lama? Kakha.* Why? Because: because reality is reality and we can't always understand why, and so we have to be humble and learn to live without final answers.

Another way of asking *Why?* is to ask *What is the purpose of life?*

Do you believe life has a purpose? If so, what is it? You need to know for yourself so you can share it with your children.

Some people tell the story, *The Purpose of Life Is*

109

to Get into Heaven, and they will link this story to the story of their religion so they can provide their children with a way to fulfill life's purpose and get into heaven.

Other people tell the story, *The Purpose of Life Is to Learn and You will Come Back to Life Until You Learn What You are Supposed to Learn*. If this is your story, you should have an answer to the follow-up question, "What am I supposed to learn?" If you have an answer for that and you share it, your child will have no need to live on to learn it, so be careful how you phrase this.

When I'm asked "What is the purpose of life?" I say this: "Life *has* no purpose; life *is* purpose." When you have something, the something you have is other than you. I have a computer, but the computer isn't me. I have an idea, but the idea isn't me. What I have is other than who I am. But I don't have life, because there is no me without life. I am life; life is me. There is nothing extra to life. Life doesn't have a purpose, life *is* purpose. You don't have to find something extra to life; you only have to live life rightly with curiosity, courage, and compassion. When you do, your heart will open and you will be filled with an ever-increasing capacity to love and be loved.

You are not here to win something, or earn something, or to escape to some other dimension. You are here to live and live well. Sure, you can choose to live backward—evil—but living forward is so much more fun and fulfilling.

When I think of the question *Why?* I often think of Buckminster Fuller. Born in 1895 (he died in 1983), Bucky was an inventor, a designer, a poet, an author, and a thinker of the first rank. But none of this matters to the question, *Why?* What does matter is this:

There came a time in Bucky's life when he wanted to commit suicide. His first child, Alexandra, had died from complications arising from polio and spinal meningitis. Years later he was broke, out of work, and a new father of a second child. He was, as he put it, a "throwaway individual." Then he had what I would call a Hillel Moment: "If I am only for myself, what am I?"

Bucky realized that his desire for suicide was fundamentally selfish. He was thinking only of himself, and how being dead would free him from the suffering of being alive. Suddenly it dawned on him that being born human meant being born with the capacity to investigate the world and perhaps find something of value to others that, if he died, would never be found. He chose to live his life as an experiment. He "saw that there was a true possibility that I could do just that if I remained alive and committed myself to a never-again-for-self-use employment of my omni-experience-gained inventory of knowledge. My thinking began to clear." His writing, however, remained somewhat obtuse.

What Bucky is saying is this: You have a unique inventory of life experiences, and from that inventory you can discover truths that can be of service to others. If you live for yourself only, or if you live with an eye to the day when you no longer live, you will ignore the value of your experience and make no effort to bring your experience to bear in the uplifting of the world. But when you live as Bucky says you should live, the answer to the question *Why are you here?* is clear: to make life better for your having lived it.

Let's put Bucky together with *Lama? Kakha*: "Why was I born?" There is no *why*, there is only the fact that you are here. "Why do I suffer?" There is no *why*, there is only the fact of suffering. Don't ask *why*, ask what shall I do with the situation in which I find myself? And here the answer is simple: you are an experiment;

you are a way life explores living; live your life as an experiment, and see what you can learn about living well, taking care of self and others. And then share what you learn with others. This is why you are here.

Summary

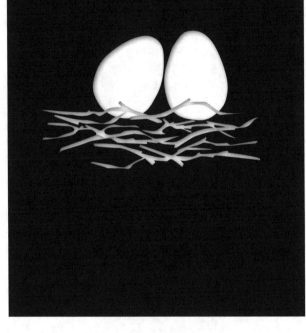

Last Words

I OPENED THE *Rabbi Rami Guide to Parenting* with the confession that I knew nothing special about being a parent. By now that should be quite evident. What I claimed to know something about was asking questions and telling stories. I still hold to that claim and hope this brief book has supported it. More than that, of course, I hope it has opened you to the power of storytelling. The stories you tell your children will form the foundation of their worldview, and that foundation will shape the quality of their lives for as long as they live.

Stories matter. Here are the five stories I urge you to tell your children in response to the five questions they will ask:

Who am I? You are a unique manifestation of life, nature, God, reality equal to and yet different from all other manifestations.

Where did I come from? You came from God (nature, life, reality) the way a wave comes from the ocean, or a rose from a rose bush.

Where am I going (when I die)? You are going back to the whole from which you came.

What am I to do (with the time between arising and returning)? Investigate life. Learn to live with curiosity, courage, and compassion. Seek out gifts to give others that will open their hearts and minds and help them do the same.

Why? Just because. It is more fun to live with curiosity, courage, and compassion than to live without them. You are here to live until you die. Live well.

Of course, these aren't stories you can pick up at a library or bookstore and read to your children; they are stories that they will learn from listening to what you say and watching what you do. But there are books you can read to your children that will help get the message across. I have mentioned some of these in the course of this *Guide*, but there are many others.

To share some of these with you, I have turned to Agapi Theodorou, a doctoral candidate in English at Middle Tennessee State University whose area of expertise is Children's Literature. MTSU is one of the few schools in the United States with this area of concentration, and Agapi is an award-winning student at MTSU. Who better to enlist in this project than her?

In the pages that follow, Agapi will list and briefly summarize both the books mentioned in this *Guide* and others of her own choosing that she feels can be of help to you in telling the kinds of stories I am promoting. I am grateful to her for her help, and certain that you will be as well.

Agapi's List:
Stories to Read to Your Children

AS A STUDENT OF children's and young adult literature, I am often asked to list my favorite picture books. More specifically, those I enjoyed as a child. My response— that I don't quite recall reading picture books—is often met with a mixture of confusion and sympathy. I hasten to add that, though I can't remember reading classic picture books, like Maurice Sendak's *Where the Wild Things Are*, I actually read quite a bit. Books on animals, and Greek fables and mythologies, and encyclopedias filled my family's bookshelves.

I was surrounded by books, but fiercely protective of one in particular: *Birds: A Guide to the Most Familiar American Birds*. My Panda bookmark still rests between pages fifty-four and fifty-five featuring the Barn and Great Horned Owls. The watercolor images of these two birds made them appear mysterious and otherworldly, unlike the parakeets I grew up with, and may partly explain my ongoing fascination with all things owl.

The same was true of the first book my father gave

me, C. S. Lewis' *The Lion, the Witch and the Wardrobe.*
Like the bird book, I explored Lewis' fantasy first
through the pictures, marveling at the strange half-
man, half-beast and the eerily beautiful queen.

It's reading experiences like these that, as Rabbi
Rami says, shape who we are. In retrospect, I can see
that my early engagement with the bird book fore-
casted my love for animals, even when that love was
sometimes misplaced, as it was when I ran up to pet a
wild donkey when I was visiting my family in Greece.
I was met with a deft kick in the butt, a sharp rebuke to
my overconfident, eight-year-old, full-of-love-for-all-
animals self. Now, leafing through the bird book (and
wincing at my phantom bruise) prompts me to reflect
on my relationship with nature. Similarly, Lucy's character in *The Lion, the Witch and the Wardrobe,* who
holds to her own truth regardless of others' skepti-
cism, reminds me of the importance of personal
integrity. In a way, I am still reading these books, even
when the books themselves are not in my hands. They
continue to shape how I perceive the world and myself
in relation to it.

The list of books (most of them picture books)
presented in the following text fosters a similar kind

119

of engagement with stories that, to quote Rabbi Rami again, "you want your children to grow into rather than out of." With that in mind, Rabbi Rami and I selected books that not only touch upon significant themes, but also encourage an active experience with words and images. This is not, however, a comprehensive list; just a starting point. I hope that these books will help you in thinking about the stories you wish to share with your children.

The key thing is to share stories that both you and your children can take pleasure in; to share stories that prompt discussion and even debate; to share picture books that make your children aware of the gaps in stories and incite them to fill those gaps with their own ideas.

What follows is an annotated list of the books mentioned in Rabbi Rami's text, along with a few additional ones that I selected. I encourage you to read these books to your kids, along with other books of your own—and your children's—choosing. Happy reading.

INTRODUCTION

Silverstein, Shel. *The Missing Piece*
Harper & Row, 1976

CHAPTER ONE: **YOU ARE A TUBE.**

Cho, Shinta. *The Gas We Pass: The Story of Farts*
Trans. Amanda Mayer Stinchecum
New York: Kane/Miller, 1994

Why do we fart? What makes some farts nauseatingly smelly and others odorless? Cho's *The Gas We Pass* answers these questions in a fun and educational manner. More importantly, however, Cho's book—part of the My Body Science series—celebrates one of the human body's natural (and necessary) functions. Rather than being ashamed of farting, we should be thankful that our tubes work so well.

Gomi, Taro. *Everyone Poops*
Trans. Amanda Mayer Stinchecum
New York: Kane/Miller, 1993

All mammals—from giant elephants and whales to teeny mice and birds—poop. Part of the fun of Gomi's picture book is reading, and re-reading, the word "poop." But there's an educational component to the text as well: it prompts readers to discuss a topic that is traditionally an awkward one, at least for Western audiences. What goes in, Gomi tells us through words and pictures, must come out, so we may as well talk about it. Defecation is a perfectly appropriate discussion topic thanks to Gomi's book, originally published in Japan, and part of the My Body Science Series.

Pollan, Michael. *Food Rules: An Eater's Manual*
New York: Penguin, 2009

In his book *In Defense of Food*, Pollan answered the question
"What should we eat?" as follows: "Eat food. Not too much.
Mostly plants." This manual breaks that mantra down into
sixty-four easy-to-read rules, or personal policies, as Pollan
likes to call them. These personal policies are meant to be
used as tools to guide our decisions about food—where we
buy it, what kinds we should eat, and how we should eat it.

From adults hoping to develop better eating habits to
children developing their food repertoires, the entire family
will benefit from this book. Above all, Pollan's manual supports "our daily lives and practices" in regard to food and
health.

CHAPTER TWO: **YOU ARE THE WORLD AND YOU ARE FROM THE WORLD/UNIVERSE**

Bang, Molly. *Common Ground: The Water, Earth, and Air We Share*
New York: The Blue Sky Press, 1997

An environmental parable, this text begins with a story of
villagers who share a common land. In time, the land's natural resources are depleted, for too many sheep have been
permitted to graze it. Bang connects this story with more
familiar contemporary ones: fishermen who try "to catch as
many fish as [they] can," and lumber companies who strip

forests bare, leaving them unrecognizable.

Bang concludes her book with a call to action and an important question. We must work together, she writes, to sustain the natural resources so vital to human life. And we must ask ourselves: in what ways can we—together—preserve our common ground? Bang's picture book can be used to ignite an ongoing discussion about environmental awareness and action.

Ehlert, Lois. *Growing Vegetable Soup*
Sandpiper Harcourt, 1987

The first book Ehlert wrote and illustrated, *Growing Vegetable Soup* engages readers through more than one narrative, as is typical of the picture book genre. The child narrator explains the process of growing vegetables with his/her father and making "the best soup ever." The pictures themselves—collage watercolors of tools and vegetables—provide readers with another narrative layer: we infer that the tools shown on each page are necessary to the work of growing vegetables.

This 1990 Parents' Choice Award Book teaches children where vegetables come from. More importantly, Ehlert's text depicts adults and children as being involved in the work of growing their food and eventually using ingredients from the garden to assemble a delicious meal. Thus the book encourages kids to see themselves as intimately connected to the food they eat.

Ehlert, Lois. *Planting a Rainbow*
HMH Books, 1988

Using the metaphor of a rainbow, Ehlert's young narrator describes, once again, the process of planting things that grow. In this text, the narrator plants a rainbow of flowers ranging from daisies to marigolds. Ehlert's characteristic style makes the flowers appear in their first-bloom best.

Ehlert also stresses the importance of waiting for the final product. It's more fun, the author implies, to wait for seeds to grow into beautiful flowers. Ehlert's books make even me, someone who loves to buy beautiful flowers from the florist's shop or the farmer's market, want to take on the more difficult job of planting my own rainbow. Here, as in Ehlert's other books, fostering an active engagement with the earth is the major theme.

Fothergill, Alastair, et al. *Planet Earth:*
As You've Never Seen It Before
University of California Press, 2007

This book features beautiful photographs of faraway places—frozen poles, great forests, threatening mountains, and big, big seas—and exotic animals like the pronghorn antelope and gelada. What's more, the authors include ample information on the places and animals highlighted in the book.

If you're searching for a text that will foster a healthy sense of awe and wonder for our planet earth, look no further. Fothergill and his collaborators photographed at locations I never knew existed and captured close-ups of animals that only local experts knew how to find. The result is a wonderful book that readers will likely return to again and again.

Love, Ann, and Jane Drake. *The Kids Book of the Night Sky*
Illus. Heather Collins
Kids Can Press, 2004

Sisters and naturalists, Love and Drake have compiled a lovely guide of the night sky, with charcoal drawings by Collins. The authors provide background information on the moon, the stars, the seasonal skies, and the planets, in addition to offering up countless projects and games inspired by the night sky.

The authors expertly blend facts about the night sky with fictional stories. In addition to learning about and exploring the solar system through interactive projects, readers may also enjoy tales about the night sky from around the world. While this book is intended for a more experienced reader, I envision even a very young child enjoying the text with some guidance. *The Kids Book of the Night Sky* certainly lends itself to collaboration and discussion.

Nivola, Claire A. *Planting the Trees of Kenya:*
   The Story of Wangari Maathai
New York: Frances Foster Books, 2008

Nivola tells the story, through beautiful watercolor illustrations and eloquent prose, of Wangari Maathai, recipient of
the 2004 Nobel Peace Prize. Maathai grew up in Kenya and
studied biology at an American college. Upon her return,
Maathai discovered her home greatly altered. Gone were
countless trees, and with them all kinds of wildlife. In hopes
of repairing the damage, Maathai urged her fellow Kenyans
to stop blaming the government for their problems and
instead to "become part of the solution."

   That solution developed into the Green Belt Movement.
In Maathai's words, it "was not simply about planting trees.
It was about inspiring people to take charge of their environment, the system that governed them, their lives and
their future." Maathai's story serves to inspire everyone—
women, men, children, inmates—to do whatever they can
to restore their homeland's natural resources.

Parr, Todd. *The EARTH Book*

New York: Little, Brown, and Company, 2010

Parr's child narrators remind us that there are so many little
things we can each do that will "make a BIG difference" in
protecting our planet. For example, we could replace plastic
shopping bags with reusable ones and turn off the faucet
when brushing our teeth. The cartoonish illustrations,

which depict children in an array of rainbow colors, lend a playful tone to Parr's book.

Like the other books in this section, Parr's text urges readers to take care of the universe so it will in turn take care of them. The earth is, after all, our home.

Seuss, Dr. *The Lorax*
New York: Random House, 1971

Dr. Seuss' *The Lorax* is a classic picture book with a not-so-subtle message. It is both a cautionary tale and a call to action, told from the point of view of an old Once-ler. Seuss' character recalls a time, long ago, when he greedily cut down all the Truffula Trees and fashioned Thneeds—"Fine-Something[s]-That-All-People-Need!"—out of them. Business was good. So good that the Lorax, who speaks for the trees repeatedly, warns the Once-ler to stop destroying the Truffula forest. The Once-ler ignores the Lorax and is soon left with no business at all, for he cut down every last Truffula Tree. The only hope for rebuilding the forest is the young boy listening to the Once-ler's tale.

As with many of Seuss' books, *The Lorax* is best read aloud. Kids will love hearing, and reciting, Seuss' sing-song language, and will enjoy his endlessly inventive talent for creating new words. Entertainment value aside, Seuss' text also warns us that, unless we care for our environment, thinking twice before taking without giving anything in return, "nothing is going to get better."

Van Allsburg, Chris. *Just a Dream*
New York: Houghton Mifflin, 1990

Walter is a litterbug. He does not recycle, even though recycling bins are available outside his middle-class residential home. And he chides his neighbor, a young girl, for watering a tree. Van Allsburg's young character has lessons to learn about how his thoughtless actions negatively impact the environment. Indeed, Walter learns by dreaming of a futuristic world in which his house is about to be bulldozed; the trees in his neighborhood are, one-by-one, cut down; and fishermen rejoice when they catch one tiny fish. Walter becomes increasingly horrified at these vivid images, and he buries his head in hopes of waking up. Walter does eventually wake up, and he's a more environmentally savvy kid.

Van Allsburg's environmental message is clear: we all have a personal responsibility toward the earth, and we must act in ways that will protect our natural resources. The book's ending supports that message, for Walter dreams of a world free of smokestacks and loggers and fisherman. Van Allsburg's assumption seems to be that environments with smokestacks and loggers and fishermen are destructive, while rural environments indicative of the past are the ideal we should work toward. This assumption should be questioned and further discussed in light of our current environmental—and technological—situation.

Lindsay, Mary, editor. *The Visual Dictionary of the Human Body*
London: Dorling Kindersley, 1991

Realistic images of the human body, paired with concise explanations, make up *The Visual Dictionary of the Human Body*. As someone interested in the subject, but not an expert in scientific discourse, I appreciated this reader-friendly text and was left more in awe of the human body.

While the book certainly celebrates the awesomeness of the human body, its illustrations are detailed, leaving little to the imagination. In short, share this book with your children only if you are comfortable with the content.

CHAPTER THREE: **YOU ARE GOD.**

Dylan, Bob. *Man Gave Names to all the Animals*
Illus. Jim Arnosky
New York: Sterling, 2010

Man Gave Names to all the Animals is Arnosky's visual representation of Dylan's song of the same name. In addition to prompting discussion of creation stories, Arnosky's realistic depictions of wild animals, hanging out all together in a primitive, jungle-like environment, are educational. Readers recognize certain animals, but are sure to learn some new ones as well.

129

To encourage that learning process, Arnosky includes a list of all 170 animals shown within the pages of the text. He then asks readers to go back and identify those creatures. If the reader does not recognize any of the names, he/she is directed to Arnosky's website. I couldn't help but look up the burro and the pronghorn, animals I've never heard of. Readers can search for these animals while listening to Dylan's CD, included on the back cover.

Zolotow, Charlotte. *Who is Ben?*
Illus. Kathryn Jacobi
Harper Collins, 1997

Zolotow's main character, Ben, seems to be entirely comfortable in his home, reading in front of a fire with his cat napping close by. Soon after, Ben ventures to his bedroom, making his way up dark stairs that appear a bit scary. The narrator's words reassure us that Ben is not afraid of the dark, a dark so potent that Ben can't even see the neighbor's house when looking outside his bedroom window. Instead, the dark inspires Ben to wonder where he was "before [he] was born." Somehow, he already knows that he was part of the blackness. He feels it. At this point, Ben's mother enters the story, and Ben asks her about the afterlife: where will he go when he dies? Surprisingly, Ben's mother has no answer. But Zolotow's character doesn't need one; instead, he feels the answer. Simply put, he's part of everything and everything is part of him.

Initially, this philosophical picture book might seem a difficult one to read to children, if only because there are no cut and dry answers. But that is what I like about Zolotow's story: it's honest. In this book, unlike in many others, the parental figure is shown to be supportive, but not all knowing, and the young character's questioning nature is encouraged. What's more, I appreciate the way Jacobi's warm, realistic illustrations make potentially scary topics— like the vastness of the universe outside our cozy homes, and the afterlife—slightly less scary.

CHAPTER FIVE: **TO OPEN YOUR HEART, STRETCH OUT YOUR HAND, BROADEN YOUR MIND.**

Durell, Ann, and Marilyn Sachs, eds.
The Big Book for Peace
New York: Dutton Children's Books, 1990

Several prominent children's authors and illustrators, including Natalie Babbitt, Lois Lowry, Maurice Sendak, Allen Say, Lloyd Alexander, and Charlotte Zolotow contributed shorts stories, poems, songs, and illustrations to *The Big Book for Peace*. According to the editors, the book's purpose is to promote peace through the stories we tell; to inspire readers to think and discuss the subject with others; and to encourage readers to create their own short stories, poems, songs, and illustrations that highlight the importance of peace.

In addition to the overall message, I appreciated the diversity of cultures and situations represented in the book. Some stories touch upon war, while others deal

131

with unhealthy family dynamics and friendships gone slightly awry. Each narrative supports the idea that we must act in ways that replace fear—of the other, of our own weaknesses, of losing status and power—with questions, dialogue, and love.

Kates, Bobbi Jane. *We're Different, We're the Same*
Illus. Joe Mathieu
New York: Random House Books for Children, 1992

Readers of Kates and Mathieu's picture book learn that people's similarities and differences should be celebrated. The author and illustrator provide snapshots that highlight individual differences: we each have distinct noses, eyes, and mouths. These pages alternate with ones that depict the characters in one unified shot, celebrating their similarities. Though we may have uniquely shaped mouths, we all use them to form words, smile, and eat. Kates and Mathieu end by reminding readers that, "We're the same. We're different. That's what makes the world such fun. Many kinds of people, not just one."

Keats, Ezra Jack. *Louie*
New York: Puffin, 2004

Susie and Roberto put on a puppet show for their friends, and everyone is shocked when Louie, the resident loner, stands up and interacts with Gussie, one of the puppets. After the show, Susie and Roberto find Louie and give the lonely boy a chance to hug Gussie good-bye.

Keats' picture book shows how Roberto and Susie figure out that what Louie really needs is the puppet. The story culminates with Louie receiving a lovely surprise, waiting for him just outside his home. Keats' book is beautifully illustrated and depicts children as compassionate and thoughtful.

Polacco, Patricia. *Chicken Sunday*
New York: Puffin, 1998

Polacco recounts growing up with her neighbors Stewart and Winston Washington, and their grandmother Miss Eula Mae Walker, in this "heart-expanding" story. Polacco considers the Washingtons to be family, even though they are very different from her own. The plot focuses mainly on how the three children plan to buy a hat for Miss Eula, a hat from Mr. Kodinski's shop that she has long admired.

The children eventually gift Miss Eula the hat, imparting joy not only to the kind, religious old woman, but also to Mr. Kodinski, the lonely hat maker. Readers have much to learn from Polacco's childhood experience, such as being aware of others' differences and learning from them; working collaboratively toward an end goal; and listening to others.

133

CHAPTER SEVEN: **BECAUSE.**

Fuller, Buckminster. *Buckminster Fuller to*
Children of Earth
Compiled and Photographed by Cam Smith
New York: Doubleday, 1972

This book compiles quotations from the American inventor Buckminster Fuller as well as selections from the film *Buckminster Fuller on Spaceship Earth*. As a result, the book does not always follow a linear narrative, which is a bit frustrating upon first reading. Yet Fuller's writing is at times poetic and always thoughtful, and it is beautifully complemented by Cam Smith's black and white photographs, which help readers to parse the book's more complicated passages.

Ultimately, Fuller tells us, we must look to nature for the "comprehensive patterns operating in the universe," and learn to live by those patterns. Like many of the books listed in the *Rabbi Rami Guide to Parenting*, this one encourages an active engagement with our world and a holistic approach to living.

Agapi Theodorou is a fourth-year Ph.D. student at Middle Tennessee State University specializing in Children's and Young Adult Literature, and Composition and Rhetoric. Agapi teaches courses in children's literature as well expository and argumentative writing. She also mentors first year teaching assistants. Besides teaching, talking, and writing about literature, Agapi loves all things owl and coffee.

ABOUT THE
AUTHOR

BORN YIRACHMIEL BEN YISROEL V'SARAH in 1951, Rami spent several years in kindergarten trying to learn to pronounce his name. Being the only first grader who had to shave, Rami was promoted through school quickly, earning both rabbinic ordination and a Ph.D. Forced to get a job at age thirty, Rami led a congregation for twenty years where he learned that irony, humor, and iconoclasm made for poor bedside manner, and honesty was rarely the best policy when it came to religion. Author of over two dozen books and hundreds of essays, Rami writes a regular column for *Spirituality & Health* magazine entitled "Roadside Assistance for the Spiritual Traveler."